Only Connect ...

Discovery pathways, library explorations, and the

information adventure.

Edited by Andrew Walsh and Emma Coonan

Innovative Libraries.

Only Connect …

Discovery pathways, library explorations, and the information adventure.

Edited by Andrew Walsh and Emma Coonan.

Print book is printed and distributed via lulu (http://www.lulu.com/), an international print on demand service, so country of printing may vary depending on country of purchase.

Paperback ISBN: 978-0-9576652-1-7

EBook ISBN: 978-0-9576652-0-0

EBook available from: http://eprints.hud.ac.uk/17339/

Published by Innovative Libraries, 2013.

195 Wakefield Road, Lepton, Huddersfield. HD1 3DH

andywalsh@innovativelibraries.org.uk

http://innovativelibraries.org.uk/

Book cover illustration and design created by Amy Kilner, http://amykilner.co.uk/ a freelance, Yorkshire based, Graphic Designer and Illustrator.

Acknowledgements

This work is primarily the work of our talented chapter authors and we're lucky to have been able to pull their contributions together and make them available here. We'd like to acknowledge the exciting, talented creations our contributors submitted to us and to thank them for their hard work in making this book a reality. We'd also like to particularly thank Amy Kilner (http://amykilner.co.uk/) who stepped in at short notice to create a wonderful cover for us! With Amy (a current student at the University of Huddersfield) doing the cover illustration for us, it was also great to see Josh Filhol (a former student of Alke - http://www.jfilhol.com/) doing the "Fishscale" illustrations.

Dedications

From Andrew ...

To Jennifer and George who love finding out new things. They have many exciting information discovery journeys ahead that I'll enjoy sharing with them.

From Emma ...

To my parents, Stephen and Ita, who nurtured my own intellectual curiosity and helped me find the tools to navigate all my journeys. (Photo courtesy of Martin O'Leary, Cobh, Ireland)

Chapter Chooser

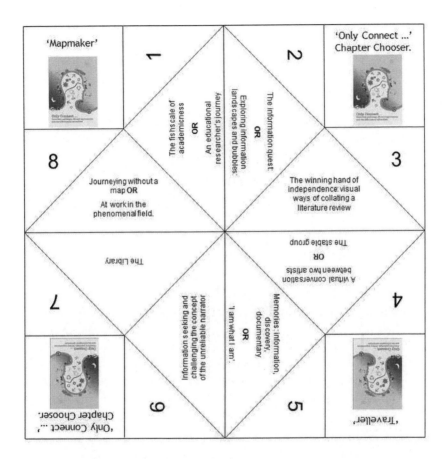

We don't intend you to read this book from cover to cover. It'd be nice if you read the introductory text first, but we won't be too upset if you don't. We'd like you to dip into the book instead and discover new things. Pick a chapter at random and see what you find – try this chatterbox to help!

1. Print or copy and cut round the outside of chatterbox

2. Fold in half and in half again

3. Open out, turn over so top is blank and fold each corner into the middle

4. Turn over and repeat so the numbers are folded into the middle

5. Turn over and slide your thumb and your finger behind 2 of outer pieces and press together so they bend round and touch

6. Turn over and repeat with the thumb and finger of the other hand for the other two outer flaps

7. The 'Only Connect …', 'traveller', and 'mapmaker' text and images should now be at the front with centres touching.

8. Decide on a word - traveller or mapmaker.

9. Make one movement of the chatterbox for each letter as you spell out that word.

10. Choose one of the numbers revealed.

11. Make that number of movements of the chatterbox.

12. Choose another number – that reveals which chapter(s) you should read next.

Table of Contents

Introduction

"The narratives of the world are numberless. Narrative is first and foremost a prodigious variety of genres, themselves distributed amongst different substances – as though any material were fit to receive man's stories. Able to be carried by articulated language, spoken or written, fixed or moving images, gestures, and the ordered mixture of all these substances … All classes, all human groups, have their narratives … narrative is international, transhistorical, transcultural: it is simply there, like life itself."

Barthes and Duisit, 1975

The origins of the book

This book came out of two frustrations of ours, but we hope it won't be a frustration for the reader.

Firstly, we were frustrated by the process of publishing itself. Most of us producing books to feed into the academic and professional publishing industry can't expect to sell many copies. The publishers understandably, therefore, want as much as possible standardised in the book production process. They can't spend the time lovingly crafting a book in the vision of the author – it simply isn't practical.

However, it **is** practical to self-publish now, which allows us as much freedom as we'd like! We can eschew commercial considerations and the need for financial profits and instead aim to primarily invest our time with relatively few costs we need to cover. Rather than fitting to pre-conceived structures we can include video; audio; images; allegorical stories; maps; whatever fits the message individual contributors want to pass on. As such the (free) electronic copy of this book is the definitive version. The print one is our best possible reflection of the richness available in the electronic copy and includes links to online content, but cannot completely echo the electronic version.

We aren't criticising the standard publishing houses. Indeed, we are likely to return to the 'traditional' route to publish work in future. However, it is relatively easy for us to self-publish works, especially non-commercial ventures like this where we expect most readers to access the material for free, with only small amount of (relatively cheap) print copies sold. This freedom also allows us to work out some of our frustrations ready for when we return to the strictures of traditional publishing houses.

The second frustration is born out of the use (or misuse) of the concept of information literacy, or perhaps the misunderstanding and misapplication of over strict interpretations.

Information Literacy

There has been much discussion around terminology; definitions and models of information literacy over the years. By and large, however, we don't have an issue about the term or the definitions that people use.

Sometimes it may make more sense to talk about individual information skills rather than information literacy (that may themselves build up to some form of information literacy), but that doesn't imply any problem with the term itself. We must also remember that information literacy is a "librarian phrase". It has meaning to library and information professionals, but that meaning may be different or absent in others. It therefore is often inappropriate to use the phrase externally, but that doesn't imply that it is not a good and usable phrase within the population it originated.

Definitions vary, but normally have the same key concepts at their core, building up to the meta-concept that is information literacy. They all give a core idea that we can build on, an idea that information literacy is about having abilities and awareness around searching out, organising, using, and communicating information.

So we agree with the phrase 'information literacy', even though we may not always use the term when describing it to others. We agree that there are many useful and relevant definitions of information literacy that we could choose.

Our frustration occurs when these definitions are built upon and applied to practice. The individual elements of a definition are taken and questions are asked "what does this actually mean?" or "how can we measure this?", which are perfectly natural questions to ask. It doesn't take long, however, before this breaking down of definitions starts to become problematic.

If we look at the sector in which the editors both work, Higher Education, the ACRL (Association of College and Research Libraries) division of the ALA (American Library Association) have detailed competency standards (http://innovativelibraries.org.uk/acrl) which have heavily influenced similar developments across the world. They contain incredibly detailed lists of competencies which they believe build up to produce an information literate student. This is echoed in similar lists for other sectors (for example, the American Association of School Librarians publish 'Standards for the 21st Century learner in action'). They feed into standardised assessment tests for information literacy such as SAILS (https://www.projectsails.org/) which claim to accurately measure the information literacy of students through multiple choice questions (https://www.projectsails.org/SampleQuestions).

Even in models such as SCONUL's 7 Pillars of Information Literacy (http://www.sconul.ac.uk/tags/7-pillars), deliberately intended to be descriptive, non-linear, and depending on context, people have built layers of competencies and details descriptors to lay over the top of this base model.

The natural tendency of many educators, librarians included, is to attempt to measure 'information literacy' as though it is a fixed, static, clear thing that exists in abstract form.

All of these take a perfectly reasonable idea or definition and abstract it to nonsense, all in the call of making them more useful. Like pinning an insect to a board for display, in fixing information literacy in such detail, they create something lacking in life and meaning. They fix a dead body in place where it can no longer interact meaningfully in any way with its environment.

Information literacy is not a fixed set of skills. Information literacy cannot be measured as a percentage or grade. Information literacy is not independent of context.

Information literacy is completely contextual. What it means to be information literate depends on how we are, what we are doing, where we are doing it. The "information literate" thing to do when "searching"; "organising"; "using"; or "communicating" information is different for a school child looking for information on the English civil war compared to a postgraduate researcher. Even within the same person, looking for information on booking a holiday, finding a builder to do some renovation work on their house, or writing a peer reviewed article will display very different ways of being information literate.

A person cannot have an objective measure of their information literacy, measured by standardised tests and marked out of 100. We cannot carry out pre and post tests around a library workshop and declare a 10% increase in information literacy because they recognise more of the library terminology. We cannot reduce a powerful concept, important for all to develop, into a list of meaningless competencies.

It is easy to make assumptions about what information literacy is, or isn't, based on our own experiences. One of us recently heard a librarian state that information literacy is dependent upon reading literacy. Unless someone is highly literate (reading fluently), then they cannot be information literate. What nonsense! That immediately assumes that verbal, visual and other sources of information contain zero information and the only relevant containers of information are written texts. If anything, we would argue that written texts are relatively minor sources of information for most people and the ability to navigate, evaluate and make sense of non-textual information sources is a much more relevant aspect of information literacy in most contexts.

The beginnings of recognizing that information literacy is contextual, rather than a static or fixed set of competencies came from Christine Bruce (1997) in her now classic information literacy book, 'The seven faces of information literacy', which was based on her doctoral thesis. This initial model, using phenomenography to describe information literacy in terms of the richness and breadth of interactions was a significant departure from previous models that used consensus and the opinions of experts to narrow down the acceptable competencies that compose an information literate person.

It has been followed by a small but growing body of relational information literacy research, recognizing the richness of real behavior rather than the primacy of any 'expert' view (e.g. Edwards, 2006; Bruce, C. Edwards, S. Lupton, M., 2006; Boon, Johnson and Webber, 2007; Williams, 2007, Bruce and Hughes 2010, Walsh 2012; Andretta, 2012).

This relational approach is the one driving our approach to this book. Instead of trying to pin information literacy down to readily measured lists of competencies, or detailed descriptions of what it means to be information literate, this book takes a different path. We take pleasure in the diversity of ways we can be information literate. The book displays many different facets of information literacy and we're pleased the individual contributors have chosen to reflect those facets in ways as diverse as 'traditional' texts; fairy story; video; graphics; and deep self reflection on learning journeys. They reflect that as information literacy has many faces, so these faces can be presented in many ways.

There is no right or wrong way to be information literate, there are simply ways that work, or don't work, for an individual in their current context. This book celebrates it and highlights a small selection of the information discovery journeys people carry out every day.

The Content

Into the woods: teaching trails and learning journeys

These pieces are remarkable individually; collectively they shed new light on the the subtle interplay between information and identity. This holds both for the roles we occupy and the relationships we construct during the processes of teaching and learning - librarian, learner, guide, seeker – and also for identity as our innermost sense of self: how we learn who we are. As Osborne writes, "How do we become ourselves - the self that we know and others recognise?" This unbook opens with the voice of the librarian-guide in dialogue with learners and other teachers, and shifts gradually towards an exploration of how our personal identities are shaped or even constituted by the information we encounter.

The two sections of this book thus offer complementary yet deeply contrasting visions of the information journey. Section One, 'The Mapmakers', presents a set of planned routes, suggested and tested by knowledgeable guides: a cross between Baedeker and Bradshaw. In this section, librarians offer a range of thoughtful observations on how learners encounter, negotiate and construct knowledge. Few of these accounts are didactic; they give not a blueprint or template for 'how to do it', but rather a topographical record of their learners' journeys.

The Mapmakers, then, offer the reassurance of well-signposted paths, including a number of 'scenic routes' or imaginative ways in which librarians and academics can help their students to choose appropriate sources of information. Delasalle and Cullen's literature search "travel guide", a collaboration between learner and librarian, is modelled as an A-Z directory of the information searching process. Gröppel-Wegener and Walton provide engaging guidelines for navigating the information ocean and identifying what you find in your fishing net, enhanced by Josh Filhol's beautiful and illuminating illustrations. Gröppel-Wegener's second contribution, which closes the section, portrays the qualitative difference between summary and synthesis through an imaginative, extended playing-card metaphor which enables learners to evaluate and collate their information 'cards' and maximise the value of their 'hand'.

Several of the Mapmakers themselves invoke and interrogate the journey metaphor. Burkhardt and Carbery's Prezi, which narrates how staff engage students in critical conversations about their information choices, is itself modelled as a learning journey from unquestioned assumption towards self-discovery. Importantly, the authors acknowledge that this journey requires learners to cross the threshold out of their "comfort zone", encountering information that may confuse or disconcert them. It's refreshing to see the emotional impact of learning acknowledged in this way, since although encountering new or contradictory information can be a deeply unsettling experience, this dimension is all too often silently omitted from information literacy discourse.

Johnson and Walsh's exploration of the information approaches of drama lecturers also highlights the affective impact of learning. Their study sees participating academics falling broadly into two groups: those who advocate "following the paths" versus those who suggest "exploring the landscape". Whereas the 'explorer' academics encourage their students to seek out new routes and new views of the subject, the path-following group focuses on getting students safely to a known information destination. Interwoven with the emphasis on safe, stable knowledge is the implication of possible divagation, disorientation or outright danger if the safe routes are departed from.

This shadowy peril is beautifully described by Linda Tolly, who maps the information journey to the template of the hero's quest. In doing so she highlights one of the most important differences between mapmaking and journeying: *the guide is not the traveller*. Not even the wisest sage (or librarian) can accompany the learner all the way on the quest, or through the dark forest. The nature of the quest is that the "travels and travails" must be undertaken by the quester, upon whom the adventures and encounters may have a life-changing effect.

Information and identity: "I am other I now"

Our second section is composed of, and by, Travellers. These authors try less than the Mapmakers to show any objective 'truth' about information literacy and show instead more of the process behind an information discovery journey in a way that as yet does not have a fixed 'lens' of information literacy imposed. Throughout we glimpse the reflective learning self which simultaneously steps into a new position and observes itself doing so: in James Joyce's words, "I am other I now". The result is candid, compelling and deliberately uneven. The authors employ a range of voices, registers and genres, sometimes within the same chapter; narratives are not brought to closure but left open, the linear sequence disrupted; the learning is ongoing.

We have represented this narrative fluidity and internal counterpoint by using contrasting fonts, but our authors have also broken out of the text-only mode to include video, audio, images, cartoons, and interactive media to both record and communicate their learning journeys. As several chapters demonstrate, the connections and associations we make between concepts are far from being exclusively textual: dialogue can take place by exchanging sound clips, artworks, doodles, dreams.

Going beyond the authority of the written word, leaving the textual path, can itself be an act of subversion that is both perilous and rewarding. As Inês Amado and Ximena Alarcón note, "the issues of migration and dislocation are always present". The two artists connect across space in a technology-mediated dialogue, which itself exceeds the bounds of the textual, to share visions and dreamscapes which combine sound, video and objects. The students in Dimmock, Hoon and MacLellan's 'Memories' go yet further, connecting across time in exploring how we encode and communicate identity through clothing and across generations.

Penny Andrews and Marika Soulsby-Kermode exchange and explore information in many media, discussing how it both assists and hampers a coming to terms with the true, autistic, self. Antony Osborne narrates compellingly the confusion of trying to construct an identity in the cross-fire of information available from scarce and conflicting sources - medical categorisation, cultural markers, the austerity of legal and judicial language, and the tacit social mores reflected (but never overtly articulated) in media representations of gay men.

There is neither library, classroom nor computer in David Mathew's study of the (deliberately ambiguous) 'stable group', yet here too the close connection between learning and identity is evident. Here learning is entirely practical and extra-textual. Horses, humans, and the author-observer all experience learning as a process of becoming, of extending the identity. Even the dogs are learning to become guardians or gatekeepers: "Zack was teaching Bonnie how to fight and to bark with more aggression".

The librarian: guide, gatekeeper, barrier?

Speaking of gatekeepers: what is the place of the librarian in these information journeys characterised by the creative, the experiential, the nontextual? A number of guide figures appear in the pages (or pixels) of this unbook, variously depicted as mentor, shaman, guardian and barrier, and helpful or sinister in about equal measure. While the mapmakers tend to represent them in a more positive light, it's evident that learners and travellers regard the librarian figure with some ambivalence!

Antony Osborne's redoubtable Mrs Fogg - a classic shusher presiding over a space smelling of furniture polish which contains none of the information he seeks - is surely related to Nick Norton's librarians, both of whom actually *withhold* information from library users whom they perceive as using it inappropriately: "No, no, now no. That is not at all what the book is for." All three are drawn from real life experiences, yet they are strangely reminiscent of the unhelpful bears and robots who staff Bryony Ramsden's fairytale library. Far from being kindly wizards, sages, or guides, these characters stand uncompromisingly between the learner and information, proffering search 'tips' along the lines of "Write a query based on a combination of base 6 numbering and binary ... (ensure interjections are in Assyrian cuneiform or C++)" (Ramsden).

At the other end of the spectrum, however, more positive visions of the librarian's potential role can be found in Johnson and Walsh's Cheshire cat, who appears at difficult forks in the path (and presumably fades away, grinning benevolently, when no longer needed); in Tolly's Sorceress-Librarian, who can gift the power of knowledge but who also recognises that the learner must quest alone; and in Norton's vision of a person-centred library entity based around the core Rogerian conditions of congruence, empathy and respect for the individual.

All these visions have in common a perception of the librarian as neither gatekeeper or shaman but as collaborator and partner in learning. They also share a vision of the library - real and/or virtual - as a space in which to create and experiment, which fosters "a joyful, playful" attitude to information (Johnson and Walsh), which perhaps even "rebrands as the Zone of Proximal Learning" (Norton).

In the journey into the unknown, creativity and learning both require an exceeding of preset boundaries. To cross this threshold is to shift into the unimagined 'now' of creativity. Signposting, guiding, and the desire to reach a place of safety give way to being playful, joyful and experimental: the positive flipside of the affective impact of information.

Stepping off the path

Teaching is developmental - it nourishes, modifies and deepens our practice and our pedagogy - but learning is transformative: it changes the learner, not the practice, and it does so at a profound level. The two processes of teaching and learning may take place at the same time (in a classroom, at an inquiry desk) yet, as Norton points out, they are "simultaneously intimate and entirely distinct". Terrain that has already been mapped is nevertheless new ground for a first-time visitor, and each newly arrived explorer steps, at every moment, into unknown territory.

The journey metaphor illustrates this slippage between the processes of teaching and learning: the contrast between retracing an established route into knowledge and the unsettling phenomenological experience of constructing the pathway for the first time. "STOP. Wait. Is that right? TRY AGAIN" (Ramsden). "I try again ..." (Cullen and Dellasale).

Our learners go where we cannot guide them. Their learning takes place in unexpected spaces and guises, away from the pathways and into the forest: exploring beyond the 'safe', known structure and into to the as-yet-undefined. As educators, we know that these metaphors represent the essence of knowledge creation, and yet we fear for our learners: we can only watch, not accompany. So we must take care that in our zeal to guide learners and help them find the right, safe pathways, we don't contain and limit or smother their intellectual journeys. We can plot a course for our teaching interventions, but we cannot predict, mandate or define our learners' journeys through information and connectivity. We can define what a 'winning hand' looks like, but we can't govern the fall of the cards. We can designate the unknown, we can even map out its extent on our charts - but that's not at all the same thing as crossing the threshold or stepping off the path.

Learning changes the learner. Whether we find the Grail or not, we have still achieved the quest: the journey itself and the information encounters we experience have effected a profound change. And who is to say when the destination is finally reached or where the journey ends? Ramsden's chapter offers us three endings out of a myriad of possilibities; and this unbook ends with an invitation to you to continue the dialogue.

We can continue to make connections between librarian and learner, between knowledge and creativity, through communicating our information encounters.

An anarcho-narrative (un)book

We initially described this book in the call for papers as being an anarcho-narrative (un)book. Our intention was to have a strong narrative element within the book. We feel this has succeeded and it has a strong element of storytelling, text that is largely descriptive rather than prescriptive, hopefully allowing the reader to make up their own minds about many of the elements.

We hope the anarchical strand running throughout it manages to stand out, using anarchy to mean the lowest possible level of organisation, such as suits the reader or author rather than the editors or publisher. Although the print format imposes an element of central rule upon the book we've tried to make it as easy to break out of as possible. The 'chapter chooser' can help decide which chapters to read next regardless of our ordering of them. The creative commons licencing and authors' retention of copyright allows contributors to re-use, re-purpose and spread their ideas elsewhere, so you may come across the same content in other places as it suits that material. The free nature of the eBook and its format as ePub rather than PDF makes it as accessible as we can make it, putting the power in the hands of potential readers.

Lastly, the acceptance of a wide range of media, rather than text plus a few images makes this an (un)book, using traditional book conventions in as light a way as we can and putting the power into the hands of our readers wherever possible. So we hope you enjoy / are challenged by / annoyed by / delighted by (delete as you see appropriate!) our first attempt at an anarcho-narrative (un)book.

References

Andretta, S. (2012). Ways of Experiencing Information Literacy: Making the case for a relational approach. Chandos: Oxford.

Barthes, R., & Duisit, L. (1975). An introduction to the structural analysis of narrative. *New Literary History*, 6(2), pp. 237-272.

Boon, S., Johnston, B., and Webber, S. (2007), "A phenomenographic study of English faculty's conceptions of information literacy", *Journal of Documentation,* Vol. 63 No. 2, pp. 204-228.

Bruce, C. (1997). *The seven faces of information literacy.* Auslib Press: Adelaide.

Bruce, C. and Hughes, H. (2010). "Informed learning: a pedagogical construct attending simultaneously to information use and learning", *Library and Information Science Research* , Vol. 32 No. 4, pp. A2-A8.

Bruce, C. Edwards, S. Lupton, M. (2006). "Six Frames for Information literacy Education", *Italics*, Vol. 5 No. 1. Available at: http://eprints.qut.edu.au/5011/ (Accessed 4th Feb 2010).

Edwards, S. (2006). *Panning for Gold: information literacy and the net lenses model.* Auslib Press: Adelaide.

Walsh, Andrew (2012). Mobile Information Literacy: a preliminary outline of information behaviour in a mobile environment. *Journal of information literacy*, 6 (2). pp. 56-69.

Williams, D. (2007). "Secondary school teachers' conceptions of information literacy", *Journal of Librarianship and Information Science,* Vol. 39 No. 4, pp. 199-212.

The Mapmakers

The Fishscale of Academicness /
Alke Gröppel-Wegener and Geoff Walton

Illustrations by Josh Filhol

Introduction: navigating the ocean and getting your feet wet

Imagine every secondary source you encounter is a sea creature!

The *Fishscale of Academicness*, inspired by the work of Dr Claire Penketh, is a visual learning idea employed to engage undergraduate students in questioning the provenance of information sources. This is an intellectual endeavour which is often absent from student researchers' academic practice (Hepworth and Walton, 2009). Developed by Dr Alke Gröppel-Wegener, the activities linked to the *Fishscale* concept aim to reduce the over-reliance on non-peer reviewed internet-based information for literature review purposes. This has been called information discernment (Walton and Hepworth, 2013) or digital judgement (Bartlett and Miller, 2011). This work was originally used with art, media and design students, who are almost by definition visual learners, but we believe this approach can be used for all learners in any context.

This chapter is based on a booklet explaining the *Fishscale* concept, and looks at the *Fishscale* from two perspectives – the view a student would have and a meta-level putting it into a larger theoretical context as a teaching activity. Therefore, it can be read on two levels: on the one hand it aims to introduce you, the reader, to the *Fishscale* concept, through clear and engaging visuals and amusing texts. On the other we have included a commentary that adds the 'academic' perspective which, in turn, enables you as learning facilitator to use the *Fishscale* concept to enable students to become information literate. So, look out for this text and the pictures, if you want to simply know about the concept, and this text if you are interested in the academic perspective.

Of course as this chapter is confined to the pages of a book, albeit an electronic one, this is only an approximation of the journey of a learner. Within the context of teaching this concept has been used to introduce students to information discernment via a lecture explaining the idea. This has then been developed further by asking the students to analyse in small groups short pieces of provided sources, to determine which sea creature they would be and explain why to the rest of the group. This prompts a discussion of where the sources would be in relation to each other on a scale of academic depth – which ones are more 'academic' sources than others. The students are then challenged to apply this strategy of information discernment to every source they include in their written assignments. Initial testing has shown that the students who had this input went on to use sources of a higher quality than in previous years.

But we are getting ahead of ourselves ... let's get started at the beginning:

Information these days seems to be everywhere. But rather than making research easier, this has made it harder, because when doing research you don't just have to find *any* information, you have to find the *right* information.

Unfortunately, information doesn't appear as a landscape, where you can see important landmarks because they rise like mountain tops.

Rather it can seem like a sea, and when you are looking for evidence to back up your research, it can be difficult to figure out what exactly goes on below the surface.

So sometimes it can feel like there is just you – on a makeshift raft – alone in a seemingly endless ocean of information.

Information literacy: launching the fishing boat

Information literacy is not a subject *per se* but a thinking skills framework which empowers learners to engage with information of any kind and which should be woven into the fabric of the subject being taught. In short, it is highly context-specific. There are many well-established models of information literacy in existence, for example those of the Association of College and Research Libraries (ACRL), the Australia & New Zealand Institute for Information Literacy (ANZIIL) and the Society for College and New University Libraries (SCONUL) 'Seven Pillars' together with some relatively new ones, for example A New Curriculum for Information Literacy (ANCIL). They all exhibit a set of core similarities which focus on the complex set of skills that learners need to find, evaluate and use information appropriately (Walton, 2009). In tandem, research done into inquiry-based learning indicates that for learning and teaching interventions to be successful they require a shift from teaching specific resources to facilitating the ability to use a set of critical thinking skills to engage with information (Hampton-Reeves et al., 2009).

Our argument, which is corroborated by work done by Levy and Petrulis (2007), is that information literacy is a fundamental building block of inquiry-based learning. Accompanied with the right kind of pedagogical intervention students' behaviours can be changed. For example, Balusek and Oliver (2012) found that by using a scale, students were able to effectively evaluate sources and correctly identify peer reviewed sources. The scale helped students distinguish between various types of sources and they found that these findings were consistent across semesters. Walton and Hepworth (2011) found that by using online discourse students can construct their own credible evaluation criteria checklist to check web-based resources and that there was evidence that students were transferring this skill into other modules.

There is wide-ranging evidence of low levels of information literacy in students attending higher education. Metzger et al. (2003) and Wiley et al. (2009) note that individuals may have trouble determining how to assess the credibility of online information. Looking at studies in the workplace in particular, Feldman (2004) reported that workers found only 50% of the information they were looking for. Workers spend 15% of their time duplicating knowledge that already exists. Breivik and Gee (2006) found that only 20% of government, 29% of commerce, 41% of news and 28% of health professionals report that they 'always' find the information they want. They estimated that undergraduates are searching approximately 0.03% of the web.

When students evaluate internet sources it has been found that they do so casually and without seeking additional verification of the information (Graham and Metaxas, 2003; Grimes and Boening, 2001; Wiley et al., 2009). In Metzger's study (2007) most participants indicated that they used these evaluation criteria 'rarely' or 'occasionally'. They also noted that they were likely to use the criteria of currency, comprehensiveness, and objectivity most often, although still only occasionally, when evaluating websites. Participants reported that they checked the author's identity, qualifications, and contact information least often. A study on young people's information behaviour (UCL, 2008 – also known as the 'CIBER Report') showed that pre-university students are unable to construct effective searches and use the narrowest of criteria to evaluate their newly-found information. They also found that users pay 'little regard to the document content' and that the 'speed of young people's web searching indicates that little time is spent in evaluating information, either for relevance, accuracy or authority…'. Finally, 'many teenagers thought that if a site was indexed on Yahoo then it had to be authoritative' (UCL, 2008). Hemig (2008, p.349) notes that artists, in particular, 'frequently cannot evaluate information that is given to them'.

Clearly there are links between the searches students do while at university and their future ability to find the right information in their subsequent workplaces. Is information literacy part of the solution of preparing our graduates for this very real workplace skill?

There are different ways to explore this endless ocean of information.

The first might be to surf. Websurfing, just as surfing the waves on the ocean, is skimming along on the surface: it allows you to cover a lot of ground, but is not in-depth.

It gets exciting once you get immersed in the material, like catching a wavetunnel and riding it for as long as you can - that is getting into the flow of research.

But there is also a chance that you could drown in a tsunami of information.

However, you won't necessarily be able to tell how deep the ocean is by skimming its top,

for that you need to explore it in more depth
 – so imagine that each of the sources you find
is a sea creature, grab a snorkel
and have a closer look!

What comes out of a 'Google trawl' can be all kinds of sea creatures – some from the shallows and some living in very deep waters.

The content here is often something that is predetermined through your search, and specifically the keywords you use. If you are typing your keywords into a search engine, lots of sources get spewed out. However, they are usually ordered by popularity, rather than the criteria you need as an academic researcher. So you have to make your own decision as to whether the source is any good for your context – and for that you have to look at the type of source you have found.

And while at the beginning you have to cast your net
wide to see what sort of sea creatures you are
turning up, once you get into finding actual sources
for your work, you need to dive deeper, to cast a
line rather than trawl with a net. You want to find
specific, not general, information and evidence.

Before we continue on our journey, we will take a moment to describe
our information literacy theoretical definition and its accompanying
model. We shall avoid rehashing all of the arguments in support of
this model but perhaps should take a moment to indicate the
underpinning research which helped to articulate and shape the model.
Chief among this is the work by Walton, Barker, Hepworth and
Stephens (2007a and b); Walton (2009); Walton (2010); Walton and
Hepworth (2011); Cleland and Walton (2012); Walton and Hepworth
(2013).

Our position on learning aligns with that of Walton and Cleland (2013)
who state that:

> [l]earning involves many things: a context such as university
> which provides a framework of roles, e.g. student and tutor,
> and associated norms, such as attending seminars and
> completing assignments; cognitive processes, such as thinking
> about something and possibly analysing and applying it;
> thinking about that analysis – reflection or metacognition;
> having feelings about the process, such as anxiety; and
> possibly changing behaviour as a result of all this, for example
> being able to make balanced judgements about a piece of
> information and use it appropriately in a given context.
> (Walton and Cleland, 2013, p.22)

In addition, because visual metaphor is central to the *Fishcale* approach,
we have found it useful to incorporate the work of Gardner (1993) who
notes that 'visual' (or more correctly 'visual-spatial') learners prefer
using images, maps and pictures to organise and communicate
information and enjoy drawing. These learners memorise by visual
association, have trouble remembering verbal instructions and are

good readers. Interestingly, this has strong parallels with the verbaliser/imager cognitive style continuum developed by Riding and Cheema (1991). On this continuum individuals are regarded as being located towards one end (imager) or the other (verbaliser) and will tend to perform better in tasks that require the associated form of information representation in memory - that is, visual or verbal (Ford, 2004). Unsurprisingly, imagers tend to prefer visually orientated information sources. Hemig (2008), in his overview of the information-seeking behaviour of artists, states that they generally favour the visual over the verbal. However, he also notes that 'textual content of print resources is more significant than previous studies suggest' (Hemig, 2008, p.349). Whilst artists are unsurprisingly visual in their learning style, therefore, they also have a significant need for textual material for their work and study. In other words, even the most visual of learners needs to engage with text at some point.

It is these issues that the *Fishscale* attempts to address.

The theory of information literacy which underpins our approach holds that becoming information literate appears to be about an individual completing a task in a given context, which frames their roles and norms (e.g., a student required to complete an assignment). This context leads to the interaction with sources (e.g. databases, e-journals, books, e-books, peers, tutors and other individuals). This interaction is defined by three 'cognitive spheres': find/access/locate; evaluate/discern/judge; use/communicate/produce. Each 'sphere' triggers an individual's behavioural, cognitive, metacognitive and affective states. It is this interplay which determines the level of new knowledge learnt (or produced or both) and the degree of changed behaviour (i.e., level of information literacy) exhibited.

All three 'cognitive spheres' appear in the *Fishscale* approach although, as you will see below, it is on information discernment that the intervention concentrates most.

When you are working with secondary sources, one of the things you have to always take into account is their provenance: Is this a good academic source? How do you know it is reliable?

There are different types of sources and some of them you should really not use as academic evidence, because they may be biased, too simplistic or plain wrong.
Whenever you are doing a literature review, this should always be in your mind - and if you are marked on the piece of research you are working on, the quality of the sources will be taken into account.

A good way of visualising this is through thinking of the research as being an ocean full of sources that are living at different depths ...

the more towards the surface they dwell,
the 'shallower' the sources are ... the further down

they are,
the 'deeper' and more theoretical they are.

To help you determine where a source belongs,
ask yourself:

**If this source was a sea creature,
what would it be like — and why?**

Would it be bright and friendly, because it has lots
of pictures in it and is easy to understand?

Would it be grey and with
dangerous teeth, because it has
no illustrations and uses
unfamiliar words?

Would it be fat, because it gives
you a lot of information on
a very specific topic?

Would it be flat, because it mentions a lot of
areas, but none of them in any depths?

Would it be puffed up, because it
seems a bit pompous and
without real point?

Would it be straight, because the information is
presented in a clear way, possibly chronologically?

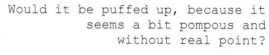

Would it be curled up,
because the information
is presented in a roundabout way?

Now that you know what your individual sources look like as sea creatures, order them onto a scale of their 'academic-ness' - are they shallow or deep? Consider what audience they were written for, their writing style and look out for clues of academic writing - referencing, footnotes, indexes, bibliographies or reference lists.

Here are some examples to get you started:

Children's books are friendly, bold, and roam very much on the surface.

Personal opinion pieces, such as blog posts, reviews or letters to the editor are usually just that: personal. That makes them less academic, because they are subjective. They also are usually short and not linked, like one in a swarm of little fish. Or they are like goldfish, little gems of amazement, but not really that substantial.

Newspaper articles are a good example of texts written for a general audience. If published in a reputable newspaper they are researched well, but they will probably show some bias. They make far reaching links and put their subjects into a larger context, but usually stop short of real academic depth as they are aimed at non-experts.

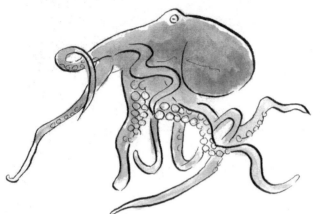

Introduct ory academic

texts, like Readers, are a good starting point, because they will get you familiar with the key ideas and debates in the field, its jargon and probably also introduce notable authors.
They tend to be flat in that they usually cover only an insight into a field of work. Some do that by concentrating on one particular issue, so they could be seen as flat horizontally.

Others give a brief introduction to a lot of issues, but don't go into much detail for each of them. In a way they are cutting through the strata of information and could be imagined as horizontally striped.

Academic overviews can take the form of a quite linear narrative, for example showing a chronological order of events – one happening after the other.
They could also be centred around a main focus, but branching into a few aspects that are discussed in detail.

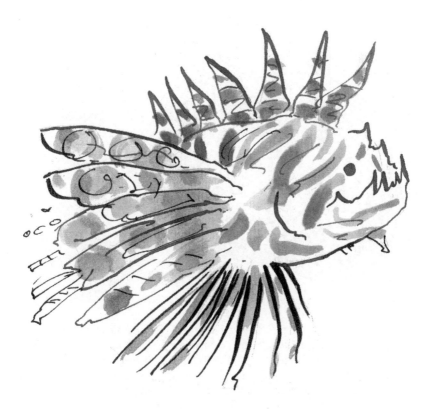

Academic texts can be quite substantial and they can seem quite a slow read – particularly if you are not used to reading at this level of depth – but keep in mind that you don't have to tackle a whole book in one sitting: rather, you could break it up into sections and summarise them in your own words – breaking down a big scary source into smaller, more easily digestible sea creatures ...

Academic texts that are found in **journals** tend to be grouped around the theme of the journal, or possibly even a special issue. Reading them can be quite daunting. If a journal is peer-reviewed that is a sign of academic depth, and these texts are often written for the expert rather than the novice. Going straight to the article might have a sting in the tail, rather pay attention to the 'safer' part of the abstract and introduction to figure out whether this text is actually going to be useful for you before you get frustrated tackling it - only to realise that it wasn't that useful in the first place.

Some academic texts might seem a bit overcomplicated - curly rather than straightforward.

Overall, academic texts should be challenging. They have teeth, which means that there should be a bit of a struggle, but getting to grips with them will be worth it in the end, because they contain good evidence.

You might also come across texts that are just too weird. They might have developed at too deep a level to make sense to a non-expert; PhD or post-doctoral work can seem that way when you are starting out in academia.
Don't get frustrated by them: if you have given it a go, carefully re-reading sections and looking up words that you don't understand, maybe they do live out of your depth for now.
Go 'back up' to find some introductory sources, which should help you establish the ideas, debates and perspectives and get you familiar with the jargon, and maybe later in your academic career you can go back down, when tackling a source in the deepest academic abyss will have become easier.

Learning to dive: understanding the information literacy and information behaviour processes involved in the Fishscale

Getting to know your fish - information discernment

The previous section forms the major part of the *Fishscale* narrative and focuses on the experiential-learning process which enables undergraduate students to become, via the use of visual metaphor, effective in information discernment. Walton and Hepworth (2013, p.55) define information discernment as "the ability to use higher order thinking skills in order to make sound and complex judgements regarding a range of text-based materials". In information behaviour terms (as illustrated by Walton and Hepworth, 2011), when using the *Fishscale*, students engage cognitively in a context-specific task defined by the roles and norms of their course, which allows them to move from an affective state of uncertainty regarding the information they are engaging with to a point of relative certainty. The use of visual metaphor not only enables students to engage in the cognitive processes of comprehending and analysing the information source (as defined by Bloom et al., 1954) in a meaningful way but also, through metacognition, triggers the act of reflection on its nature. In this way it helps the student to produce new meaning, and hence new knowledge, about the source in question.

By posing a series of questions which use highly descriptive words to create a visual image of the text-based information source, this concept enables the learner to think of the (secondary) source in a new and amusing way and so may change their affective state in a positive way. In so doing what can be a highly negative and stressful process – evaluating academic information sources – changes into the amusing and enjoyable task of visualising those sources as a certain kind of fish or sea creature. The added group activity of physically designing/drawing those creatures then makes the process of questioning provenance even more memorable. The questions suggested offer different ways of visualising the sources to make it easier to make judgements about them: e.g. would a resource with lots of information be fat? Is it curled up like a sea horse because the information is presented less clearly than a more straightforward narrative, which would be represented as a straight fish like an eel? The *Fishscale* enables the reader to make a series of judgements using metaphor to create a way of visualising the analysis.

The series of examples given also enable the reader to create a mental and visual hierarchy of the sources in question through the added dimension of the notion of depth. Thus the more scholarly the resource, the 'deeper' its *Fishscale* metaphor lives in the ocean, while the less credible resources live in the 'shallows'. Again, this takes the abstract notion of the 'academic' and allows students to visualise it, ordering a number of sources on a scale in order to see them in relation to one other.

The *Fishscale* narrative spends some time giving examples of visual metaphor which enable learners to apply their analysis to the source, reflect on the result and devise a hierarchy of resources to use in their assignments. Almost every conceivable text or resource that a first-year student would be exposed to is given in the narrative, which provides a clear set of templates for learners to work with. This enables them to understand the character of a source, interact with it and use it with other sources to synthesise into their assignment.

> At the beginning of a research project, you probably have to cast your net wide, and establish your focus by looking at introductory sources; but once you have come up with your focus, a research question and key words for a literature search, you will be able to cast a line at the academic depth that you want to dive down to.

Casting your net - finding information

Although we recognise that artists in particular are resistant to library instruction, preferring open browsing and mediation from experts (Hemig, 2008), we also subscribe to the view (corroborated by empirical research in Walton and Hepworth, 2011; 2013) that information behaviour can be changed and information literacy enhanced.

When students can visualise what information they need for their assignments, they can become more effective searchers. The metaphor of fishing is extended in the sense of casting one's net wide, so the search is as broad as possible but focused by using the most appropriate keywords. Alternatively, their search can be very focused by casting a line (keyword search string perhaps) into the depths.

```
Keep in mind when you are writing up your own
project that this work could also be seen as a sea
creature, and that there are types you should
avoid:
Avoid giving a collection of facts that are not
really linked. A paragraph on something interesting
you learned followed by another paragraph on
something interesting you learned is only
```

interesting if you can properly link those paragraphs in a meaningful way.

You should usually try not to write an essay that is just a list of things one coming after the other. While this might work when you are required to write something based on a chronological structure, it usually ends up being a summary and shows little of your own skills of analysis.

While of course you want to show off all the reading that you have done, don't be tempted to just make your writing about quoting the exotic seeming things that you have read, an essay full of quotes, while proving that you have done some research, does not show your skills at highlighting *what* is important in what you have found out and *why* that is important.

What you should be aiming for is a well-rounded piece of research that has a strong focus.

What's on the menu? Using information

The *Fishscale* ends by giving advice on using information and provides a template for sharing knowledge. It very clearly states the need to avoid listing but rather to synthesise knowledge from found sources into a new whole. In addition, the notion of reflecting on work done is promoted, which is a useful means for securing learning. In this way the student is more likely to create new knowledge - not necessarily ground-breaking but new to him or her - which stretches beyond the mundane to something worthwhile and interesting.

Conclusion: back to dry land

We are not suggesting that this form of pedagogical intervention using visual metaphor will turn everyone into outstanding discerners of information, but we do believe it will help many, especially those who tend to have a more visual learning style. This approach also supports the need to use a variety of teaching and learning interventions to engage as many learners as possible, whatever their learning style. What makes this work so well is, as this analysis demonstrates, that the *Fishscale* not only engages many of the cognitive states required to enhance learning but also the metacognitive and affective states, which means it is ultimately more likely to succeed. The *Fishscale* is an addition to, not a replacement for, the rich variety of pedagogical interventions that educators, including librarians, use to enable learners to gain the attributes required to become information literate.

We are continuing our research on the *Fishscale* to determine whether it transfers to different setting and subjects, which is going to be exciting and interesting. All we can say is: watch this space!

References

Balusek, K. & Oliver, J. (2012). *An assessment of students' ability to evaluate sources using a scale.* International Society for the Scholarship of Teaching & Learning (ISSOTL) conference held at Hamilton, Canada 22 - 27 October.

Bartlett, J. & Miller, C. (2011). Truth, lies and the internet, a report into young people's digital fluency. London: Demos. [Online] http://www.demos.co.uk/files/Truth_-_web.pdf (accessed 18 July 2013)

Bloom, B. S., Engelhart, D., Furst, E. J., Krathwohl, D. A. and Hill, W. H. (1956). *Taxonomy of educational objectives: the classification of educational goals: handbook 1: cognitive domain.* New York: David McKay Company Inc.

Breivik, P. S. & Gee, E. G. (2006). *Higher education in the internet age. Libraries creating a strategic edge.* Westport: Praeger.

Cleland, J. & Walton, G. (2012). Online peer assessment: helping to facilitate learning through participation. *Journal of Learning Development in Higher Education, 4*

Feldman, S. (2004). The high cost of not finding information. *KM World Magazine,* March 1. [Online] http://www.kmworld.com/Articles/ReadArticle.aspx?ArticleID=9534 (accessed 19 March 2008).

Ford, N. (2004). Towards a model of learning for educational informatics. *Journal of Documentation,* 60 (2), pp183-225.

Gardner, H. (1993). *Frames of mind: the theory of multiple intelligences. (2nd edn.).* London: Fontana Press.

Graham, L., & Metaxas, P.T. (2003). "Of course it's true; I saw it on the Internet!" Critical thinking in the Internet era. *Communications of the ACM, 46*(5), 71-75.

Grimes, D.J., & Boening, C.H. (2001). Worries with the Web: A look at student use of Web resources. *College & Research Libraries, 62*(1), 11-22.

Hampton-Reeves, S., Mashiter, C., Westaway, J., Lumsden, P., Day, H., Hewertson, H. and Hart, A. (2009). *Students' Use of Research Content in Teaching and Learning: A report for the Joint Information Systems Council (JISC).* [Online] http://www.jisc.ac.uk/media/documents/aboutus/workinggroups/studentsuseresearchcontent.pdf

Hemmig, W. S. (2008). The information-seeking behavior of visual artists: a literature review. *Journal of Documentation,* Vol. 64 Iss: 3, pp.343 – 362.

Hepworth, M. and Walton, G. (2009). *Teaching information literacy for inquiry-based learning.* Oxford: Chandos.

Levy, P., and Petrulis, R. (2007). *Towards transformation? First year students,inquiry-based learning and the research/teaching nexus.* In: Proceedings of the Annual Conference of the Society for Research into Higher Education (SRHE), 11-13 December 2007, Brighton, UK.

Metzger, M.J. (2007). Making sense of credibility on the Web: Models for evaluating online information and recommendations for future research. *Journal of the American Society for Information Science and Technology, 58*(13), 2078–2091

Metzger, M.J., Flanagin, A.J., & Zwarun, L. (2003). College student Web use, perceptions of information credibility, and verification behavior. *Computers & Education, 41, 271–290.*

Riding, R.J. and Cheema, I. (1991), "Cognitive styles – an overview and integration". *Educational Psychology,* Vol. 11, pp. 193-215.

University College London (2008). *Information behaviour of the researcher of the future: a CIBER briefing paper, executive summary.* [Online] http://www.ucl.ac.uk/slais/research/ciber/downloads/ggexecutive.pdf (accessed 19 March 2008).

Walton, G. (2009). *Developing a new blended approach to fostering information literacy.* Unpublished PhD Thesis: Loughborough University.

Walton, G. (2010). *From online discourse to online social networking, the e-learning Holy Grail?.* **In** Parkes, D. and Walton, G. (eds.). *Web 2.0 and libraries: impacts, technologies and trends.* Oxford: Chandos, pp33-65.

Walton, G., Barker, J, Hepworth, M., Stephens, D. (2007). Using online collaborative learning to enhance information literacy delivery in a Level 1 module: an evaluation, *Journal of Information Literacy, 1* (1), pp13-30.

Walton, G., Barker, J, Hepworth, M., and Stephens, D. (2007). *Facilitating information literacy teaching and learning in a level 1 Sport & Exercise module by means of collaborative online and reflective learning in the Blackboard virtual learning environment (VLE).* **In** Andretta, S. (ed). *Change and challenge: information literacy for the 21st century,* pp169-202.

Walton, G. & Cleland, J. (2013). *Strand 2: becoming an independent learner.* **In**, Secker, J. & Coonan, E. (eds.). *Rethinking information literacy: a practical framework for teaching.* London: Facet.

Walton, G. and Hepworth, M. (2011). A longitudinal study of changes in learners' cognitive states during and following an information literacy teaching intervention. *Journal of Documentation* 67 (3), pp449-479

Walton, G. & Hepworth, M. (2013). Using assignment data to analyse a blended information literacy intervention: a quantitative approach. *Journal of Librarianship and Information Science,* 45 (1) pp53-63

Wiley, J., Goldman, S., Graesser, A., Sanchez. C., Ash, I., & Hemmerich, J. (2009). Source evaluation, comprehension, and learning in internet science inquiry tasks. *American Educational Research Journal, 46,* 1060-1106.

An Educational Researcher's Journey / Mairi Ann Cullen and Jenny Delasalle

This chapter follows a search journey in seven parts carried out by Mairi Ann Cullen, a researcher at the University of Warwick's Centre for Educational Development, Appraisal and Research (CEDAR). This particular journey took place in April 2011 but the principles employed along the way will be of relevance across the disciplines and across the years. Within each part of the journey, the literature search principles exemplified have been described by Jenny Delasalle, at the time a Librarian at the University of Warwick with a remit to support researchers.

Our researcher's journey is described in seven parts, and the librarian's search principles form a list as long as the alphabet, so a kind of A-Z guide [http://www.az.co.uk/] to literature searching grows from one individual's journey. The librarian's principles are tips that researchers from other disciplines might also find useful, so this chapter works rather like an illustrative travel guide.

Mairi Ann Cullen's original blog posts [http://innovativelibraries.org.uk/MA1] and [http://innovativelibraries.org.uk/MA2] are available on the University of Warwick's 'ResearcherLife' [http://blogs.warwick.ac.uk/researcherlife/] blog.

Part one: Where I've come from

I listened and learned from Principal Investigators (PIs) and colleagues about creating a literature search template and defining a set of limits. They taught me that it was imperative to keep a running note of how I was going about the process so that I could later describe what I had done. As time and technology went by, I picked up some cursory knowledge about literature searching online.

Recently, however, I've become more aware of just how cursory this knowledge was – I knew I wasn't getting the most out of the search tools available and turned to the Library staff for help.

Today, I'm going to begin to put into practice what I've learned so far from Chris Bradford and Jenny Delasalle, Academic Support staff in the University of Warwick Library [http://www2.warwick.ac.uk/services/library/]. Most importantly, they taught me that it's worth learning how to use each specific database that is relevant.

Part one: Literature Search Principles

A. When you're already familiar with all the relevant articles you find, then it's time to stop searching.

B. Follow the reference trail: when you find a good article, look at the papers that it cites.

C. Take advice from experienced researchers.

D. Keep learning throughout your career: the search tools available to you will keep evolving.

E. Library staff will be up to speed with the latest search tools and techniques, so take their advice and tips.

F. Explore all the databases of relevance to your research.

Part two: My literature search launch

Today I'm starting to search for literature to situate a draft article on which I'm joint, but not lead, author. My task at this stage is to place our findings and our argument in the relevant literatures around parenting styles, anti-social behaviour, social class, and social policy. I'm familiar with the literature on parenting styles so I'm going to start with literature on anti-social behaviour.

First stop, of course, the Library homepage – I clicked on Resources, then selected my Subject as 'Education' (I'll start there but I plan to come back later and try again by selecting 'Social Sciences – all subjects') and my E-resources as 'Databases'. These choices take me to the reassuring Education resources page with the photo and contact link for our Academic Support Librarian, Chris Bradford. I know that I can ask her for help if I get myself lost in the literature searching minefield.

I select 'Key electronic resources for Education' which takes me to the recommended set of relevant databases. I scan the list and, at this stage decide to ignore the 'key list' and go for the wider remit of ASSIA (Applied Social Sciences Index) as I suspect my search term, 'anti-social behaviour' is not Education-specific. The **CSA Illumina search page** opens up. Having benefited from a conversation about literature searching with Jenny Delasalle, I'm aware of the need to learn a bit about each database as I use it so I take advantage of the option to click on 'search tips' before I launch off on my own.

Part two: Literature Search Principles

G.   Be clear about the purpose of your literature search before you begin.

More on this: Setting your own work in context, exploring a new topic, finding literature from other disciplines, carrying out a systematic review all require different approaches, amounts of time and record-keeping practices. You will need to follow an approach suitable to your own discipline and needs.

H.   Be precise about the topic(s) you wish to explore.

More on this: For ideas of possible ways to refine your search topic, visit the advanced search form on the database you are searching: what elements could be useful to you? Refinement ideas might come to you as you handle the literature that you find. See Part three of this journey, where Mairi Ann explains her topic more precisely; Part four, where she is reminded to focus her research on Britain in particular; and Part five where she recognises the danger of side-tracks.

I.   Find out what resources are recommended for your discipline by your library website or librarian.

J.   Note the difference between the database or source of information (in this case, ASSIA) and the search platform or tool you are using (in this case CSA Illumina).

More on this: See also Principle M, know your database or source. Some platforms will allow you to search many databases at one time, and some databases are available on more than one platform (eg 30+ interfaces for PubMed to search MedLine). This can make it worth your while investigating which databases are of interest to you, and which platforms you can use to search those databases: one particular platform might save you time by bringing you results from a number of databases. However, you often get the most specific search/refinement options when searching one database at a time, so if you are getting too many results then it might help to search only one database at a time.

Also see Principle Q: you should know what elements of an article a keywords search will be searching through.

K.   Use the database's or tool's own 'search tips', or 'help', or guides, to learn how to get the best from that particular database.

More on this: Often, you can find bite-sized explanations and tips behind elements of a search page from links on the search page itself. When you want to use wildcard, truncation or phrase searching (see Principle O in Part four and Principle R in Part five), you need to know how to express those in the characters recognised by that database.

Part three: CSA Illumina search tips considered

Below, in bold text, are the first three tips on CSA Illumina's 'Tips for successful searching' page (from 2011), along with my responses:

Before building your search, ask yourself the following questions:

1. What information are you looking for? Consider stating this in writing in two or three sentences.

Articles published on anti-social behaviour (at least since 1997 when New Labour government elected); would be good to know when and why this term was coined and what exactly it means so articles defining and/or critiquing the term would be useful; in particular I need to find articles that provide empirical evidence for predicting who is 'at risk of' this type of behaviour, and also articles about interventions around anti-social behaviour, including parenting programmes.

2. Identify general concepts about the information that you're looking for, and ask how they might relate to the search terms that you might use.

General concepts around anti-social behaviour? Opposite might be 'pro-social behaviour'. Similar terms might include 'conduct disorder', juvenile delinquency', 'offending behaviour', 'juvenile offending'.

3. Are you interested in a specific author's work? If so, then that might be a very good place to start. You might use articles by this author to discover other relevant documents to satisfy your research needs.

I used to think this approach was 'cheating' and not a 'proper' literature search strategy, but here it is recommended on a database site. This approach was also recommended by Jenny Delasalle so, after all these years of thinking I was doing it wrong somehow, I feel vindicated about starting from one known piece of the literature and launching off from there. However, I'm keen to gain a feel for the field beyond what I know already so I've noted this tip but it's not where I want to start today.

Part four: CSA Illumina's journal coverage and ASSIA

The fourth search tip on CSA Illumina (in 2011) says:

Are there specific journals that publish articles related to your subject? You might want to take a look at the serials source lists attached to each database's factsheet (the factsheet appears as an '?' button next to each database name).

This sounds interesting. I try following the '?' next to the database name, I click on 'selected databases' and there ASSIA comes up as the first one so I click on the '?' beside it. Wow! Now that does bring up useful information, including subject coverage, dates of coverage (from 1987) and, over on the left-hand side, Serials Source List and an ASSIA database guide. I click on the serials source list and up comes a long list of all the journals included in this database. Some, including some that I've never heard of before, do look as if they might cover my topic of 'anti-social behaviour'. Here are a few – and only one of these is familiar to me:

- Aggression and Violent Behavior, 1359-1789, Core

- Aggressive Behavior, 0096-140X, Core

- Behavioral Sciences & the Law, 0735-3936, Core

- Behavioral Sleep Medicine, 1540-2002, Core

- Behaviour Research and Therapy, 0005-7967, Core

- Emotional & Behavioural Difficulties, 1363-2752, Core

- Environment & Behavior, 0013-9165, Core

- Ethics & Behavior, 1050-8422, Core

As I go down the list, I feel overwhelmed – there could be an awful lot of literature out there on this topic! But just looking at the two ways 'behaviour' is spelled has reminded me to refine my search to articles published in Britain, thus excluding much of the American literature on 'behavior' at least in the first instance.

Looking at the ASSIA Database Guide document is also very useful. (I printed it off. I'm hard-copy at heart!) It states that it's designed for the information needs of the caring professions and focuses on the practical problems of society. It covers education, as well as health, social sciences, psychology, sociology, economics, politics and race relations. It sounds spot on for my quest – the draft article is about parenting programmes targeted at parents of 8-13 year olds at risk of anti-social behaviour. I'll read on and see what else I learn.

More good stuff in this Guide – I learn that ASSIA content is drawn from journals of which about 46% are published in the UK (43% in USA) so that's good for my search needs. I also learn that it is recommended to use the database Author Name Index for author searches and to use its Thesaurus for search term Descriptors. I remember now that Chris Bradford recommended that during a session I attended but I'd forgotten until reminded again today. I learn that the Keywords field in ASSIA is used to search the Abstract, Descriptors and Title – that's useful to know. In fact, the whole Guide (15 pages with permission to copy) is full of exactly the information I need to go ahead with my search, including how to narrow or extend a search. I'm ready to give it a whirl.

Part four: Literature Search Principles

M. Know your database or source. Which journals are covered, for what dates?
<u>More on this:</u> Some journals are covered in multiple sources but not always for the same dates. See also Principle J: you should know the difference between a source or database and a search platform that is the tool used to search. Also learn whether the database you are searching is an abstracting and indexing one, or a full text one: this is discussed here in Principle W, in Part five.

N. Consider searching for or within particular journals, especially if you know titles that are relevant.

More on this: Note that the lists of journals in a database can also be useful for authors. Journals that are indexed in the places where you search are likely to be good places for publication, to reach researchers like you.

O. Allow for spelling variations, eg American/British, plurals, hyphenated words: wildcard symbols may help.

More on this: Spelling variations can help you to either narrow or widen your search. To widen your search, consider using wildcard and truncation symbols. You should read about the appropriate symbols for wildcard or truncation searching to use in the database that you are searching. For example, Proquest [http://proquest.umi.com/i-std/en/lcd/ref/wild.htm] has a guide. There is more on this principle in Part five of this journey.

P. Look for an index or a thesaurus that you can browse, to find the terms most relevant to you.

Q. When you put your keywords into a simple search box, consider what you are searching through: full text or certain parts of a record?

More on this: In some databases you are searching the records describing journal articles, as with the database that Mairi Ann writes about. In others you might also be searching the full text of an item (as when you search Google Books), or through the references cited by articles that are indexed.

Part five: Some results

I decide to try first with Advanced search. I follow advice and look up the database Thesaurus. Good job I did because anti-social behaviour is 'Not found' – the form used is spelled without the hyphen. Also I find out that there is a long list of 'behaviour' words. I must be very focused and not get side-tracked into a jungle of by-ways, searching everything ever written on 'behaviour'! I decide to start as simply as possible by searching 'Anywhere' for 'antisocial behaviour' AND (England, OR Britain OR United Kingdom), limited to 'journal articles only' and 'English only'.

This yields 267 scholars and 161 peer-reviewed journal articles. A quick glance down the first page of the list shows that I need to refine my search further. I go back and add in 'parent*'. This takes it down to a more manageable 44 peer-reviewed articles.

I scan through this list, clicking to select any that seem relevant. Sometimes I click on 'View Record' if the short form information on screen is not quite enough to decide whether or not the article is relevant. Then I 'Return to Results' to get back to the list. I end up with 34 'Marked Records' and am able to save this and choose what to do with it in another window – but first I clicked on 'Please log in to My Research'. I sign up and create a profile. I'm hoping this means that, next time I use this database, I'll be able to find this particular search for reference. Just in case, though, I elect to save my marked records to a folder on my computer.

This next bit takes me a few hours but I don't know how to shorten the process. I go to my 'Marked Records' list and click on 'View Record' for each one. This takes me to 'Record View'. Here I can click on 'WebBridge' to get to the full article electronically. I choose to save the ones I'm really interested in as PDFs on my computer to read and refer to later. I notice that there are lots of options available – e.g. to set up e-mail alerts to particular journals as new articles or new issues come out or to set up RSS feeds - but I decide to try to focus on my literature search and to note these possibilities for exploring more another time. One that I do use, though, is the option to look up articles that have cited the article I'm interested in. This doesn't always lead to relevant articles for me but it does lead to a few that perhaps I wouldn't have found easily otherwise. I save these too. I notice that it takes quite a bit of concentration to remember which windows I can close (e.g. to get back out of a particular journal webpage, and back out of the WebBridge window) and which I need to take care to use 'Return to linked references'. I use the 'Next' and 'Previous' buttons on the screen to navigate through the records.

As I'm going through this process for my 34 Marked Records, I learn more and more as I go. For example, each Record View shows Descriptors for that article and I can see that some of these would be useful if I dare to edit my search any further.

For example I could experiment with using Descriptors such as 'Interventions' or 'Risk factors' or 'socioeconomic status' but I decide not to as my consuming fear throughout all of this time is that I will drown in a sea of apparently endless relevant literature. I need to keep remembering that all I am trying to do is to learn as quickly as I can enough about what is out there to 'place' our contribution appropriately in the field.

I learn that some journals carry more than one article that is particularly relevant to my interests and so I note these and plan to search only these journals another time. I also find that one journal, the BMJ (British Medical Journal), seems very relevant but is not available on WebBridge nor in our own Library (which can be accessed using 'search catalogue'). I note that I need to Google that journal's own website in order to access all my Marked Records from the BMJ.

Part five: Literature Search Principles

Note the example of a truncation symbol in this search: 'parent*': see Principle O in Part four, and remember the constant need to apply Principle G (Part two), knowing what you intend to achieve: don't get side-tracked!

R. Combine two related concepts with 'OR' and two different concepts with 'AND'.
More on this: Many databases work like Google, in taking an implied 'and' between keywords. Therefore if you mean to search for a phrase, you may have to use quotation marks or similar, around the phrase. Combining words in this way is sometimes called Boolean searching, and one good guide to Boolean searching is available on the MIT Libraries' site. [http://innovativelibraries.org.uk/MIT] Note in Part six that ASSIA's own guide also explains Boolean searching.

S. Aim for no more than 60 results.
More on this: Sixty is probably the maximum number of results that you will want to read through and select for further investigation. When you have more results than you can handle, refine your search by adding another element to your query. When you have too few results, take out an element of your search query.

T. Create an account and save a list of articles to explore later.
More on this: You may need to create a personal account that you log into separately, after you've already logged in through the authentication process. Use personal accounts to store searches and set up e-mail alerts when new items are added to a database that match your search query, as well as to store lists of interesting articles.

U. Keep records so that you can find your way back again if you get lost amongst the literature.
More on this: If you definitely want to change your search topic or the purpose of your searching time, then make a record of how far you got on the original topic and then define your new topic thoroughly from the beginning. (NB, in Part seven, Mairi Ann uses a handy template for recording keywords for each topic.) Literature searching is a journey and you need to keep referring to your directions, and to mark where you've been on your map! You could create a spreadsheet (PhD students could turn this into a thesis appendix) and record in it some or all of the following elements:

- name of the resource searched, eg ASSIA, on CSA Illumina

- date of your search, eg April 2011 (Keeping up to date: date search was re-run? Email alert set up?)

- Keywords and limits used (for each search)

- Number of results for that search

- Login details or clues about them, for your personal account on that database: in addition to your spreadsheet, do make sure that you save any useful searches or search history, on your personal account

- Notes on how useful you found the database, the kinds of results you found, etc.

- Tips for yourself on how to search on that database.

Another recording idea is to print out a copy of your search history when you have finished searching: you can scribble any notes, tips or ideas on the print-out.

Some reference management software enables you to record how you found items that you add to your collection.

V. Back everything up! It takes a long time to perform such searches, so don't risk losing track of what you've done and found.

W. Click on links to find the full text of articles, or search the library catalogue.
<u>More on this:</u> WebBridge is the University of Warwick's OpenURL resolver, and many other libraries use one called 'SFX'. OpenURL resolvers are not 100% reliable, as in this example where Mairi Ann could not access BMJ content. The University of Warwick's Digital Access Manager, James Fisher, commented on the original blog post: "As you have found, this tool often helps to link you to the full-text of articles that we subscribe to. However, sometimes it is not able to do this. This may be because we don't subscribe to the journal. However, it can also sometimes be due to the information that is passed to WebBridge by the database that you are using. WebBridge tries to interpret this data and check whether we have access to an article. If this data is unclear this may result in WebBridge being unable to check our holdings. For this reason, if you find an article that looks really relevant which WebBridge is unable to find it could still be worth checking the Library Catalogue to see if we do subscribe to it."

X.   To do a literature search properly, allow plenty of time and shut out distractions.
<u>More on this:</u> For a search eliciting 60 results, ideally you should allow three hours for defining your topic, searching the database, refining your search, recording your searching and investigating articles of interest. You will then need to allow more time to read the articles that you've found, as we see in Part seven.
It is quicker to find the full text when searching in a full-text database than in an abstracting and indexing (A&I) database such as ASSIA, which Maira Ann searched. You could search the full-text databases first, but unless they are specifically relevant to your subject area they might not include key journals for your research, so you'd have to search in the A&I database as well, and then you'd need to spend time eliminating records you already know about from your A&I results - so I would recommend starting with the database most relevant to your research in the first place, whether it is full-text or A&I.

Y.   When navigating within a database, it is often safer to use the database's 'next' and 'previous' buttons than your browser buttons.

> More on this: By using the database's internal navigation buttons your browser won't have to send your query to the database again, taking time and potentially stalling, and you won't go back past a stage at which you selected an article for your list, before the database has registered your tick!

Part six: Next steps in my literature search

Having started searching, I refer back to the advice on the CSA Illumina Search tips page: their text appears in bold here.

5. After you've located a couple of relevant documents, consider using the descriptors attached to the record to locate similar records.

I considered this: see Part five. This would be a useful way of extending a search if the initial search came up with a very small number. With my 30-plus Marked Records, I have more than enough on my plate!

Need further assistance? Talk to your institution's reference librarian or take a look at our quick reference card and other search related articles:

- **Quick Search**

- **Advanced Search**

- **Boolean Operators (including proximity searching)**

- **Wildcard Characters**

All these topics are covered in the ASSIA Guide, which I printed off and read.

Now I need to stop searching and read some articles. As I do that, I'll be trying to piece together a rough shape for the literature in this field – what are the key concerns? How do they relate to each other? Once I have a rough sense of that, I'll decide where next to take my search. I'll keep posting as I go.

Part six: Literature Search Principles

Z.   If you find only a few results, use subject headings, keywords or descriptors in an article's record to explore wider or related topics. More on this: Subject headings, keywords or descriptors in the records of the results are often hyperlinked searches, so can be quick to investigate.

Part seven: Complex search strings!

Yesterday, I did some reading and followed up some of the references in these articles to add to my electronic pile. I'm beginning to create a rough draft of a mental 'knowledge object' in my head. I even had a go at drawing it out on the blackboard in my office.

Today, I've decided to search for some more literature about parenting programmes as social policy. I go back to ASSIA and create a new search. To help me, I make use of the Search Strategy template given to me by Jenny Delasalle [http://blogs.warwick.ac.uk/libresearch/entry/creating_a_search/] which helps me to think of cognate concepts for 'parenting programmes' and 'social policy'. I decide on (social OR public OR education*) AND (parent*) AND (program?s OR intervention*), limited to (UK OR United Kingdom OR Britain).

That came up with no journal articles so I review that search and decide to take out the AND (program?s or intervention*) line and try again. I try various edits of this search but I get no journal articles coming up. Clearly, I'm doing something silly.

I try again. I go for (social OR public) AND (policy) AND (parent*) AND (England OR United Kingdom). This time, I get 213 peer-reviewed articles. I need to narrow this down to those that are about parenting programmes so I edit the search by adding AND (training OR program?? OR intervention). This produces 55 peer-reviewed articles. I scan through these, clicking the tick box for those I think are relevant. Only 11 are.

I think I've still not got the search terms as neatly defined as I'd like so I try again, this time with (social policy) OR (public policy) AND (parent* program??) OR (parent* training) OR (parent* intervention)

AND (England OR United Kingdom). This time I get one solitary article and it's one of the previous 11. I'm perplexed – I know this can't be right. Ah, lightbulb moment. I go back to the articles I was reading yesterday and look at the keywords they used. Instead of 'social policy' they have been really specific and used 'parenting orders'; instead of 'parent programmes', 'training' or 'interventions', one article has used 'parenting support'. I try again ...

The Librarian's concluding comments

Now we are reminded of the very first principle in Part one of this journey: when you already know the results you are finding, then it's time to stop searching. Perhaps our researcher could move on to try her search queries on other databases (Principle F in Part one). We can also see how literature searching is not linear but made of many circles, as the articles that you find suggest ways to define your topic or refine your search further.

What this final part of the search journey shows is that our researcher is tenacious, patient and resourceful, which will no doubt be good qualities for other aspects of research beyond literature searching!

The Researcher's concluding comments

This journey exploring online tools for literature searching has taught me useful principles that I have applied in all my searches since. The article on which I was working will be published in the *British Educational Research Journal*, volume 39, number 6, in December 2013. It is available online – DOI: 10.1002/berj.3020 (http://onlinelibrary.wiley.com/doi/10.1002/berj.3020/abstract)

The Information Quest: Mapping the Information Adventure to 'The Hero's Journey' of Joseph Campbell's Monomyth / Lynda Tolly

Does it ever feel as though some students find themselves lost in the midst of their information-seeking travels and travails? They seem tired and weary from seeking the elusive Holy Grail of research – the resources that will work best with their current research needs and help them achieve that stellar paper or project. Too often, errant students wander aimlessly, misguided along the path of their own wayward information quest. In a sense, they become the heroes in their own quest narrative, but as with all quests, heroes often find mentors and guides along the way to help them conquer the multiple tests and challenges they face before they can reach their journey's end and return home triumphant with their hard-earned GPA intact. Thus, the information seeking process can oftentimes seem like the quest of the 'Hero's Journey' as described by Joseph Campbell in his seminal work *The Hero With a Thousand Faces*.

Campbell's Monomyth

Ever since mythologist Joseph Campbell plotted the hero's journey onto the archetypal monomyth in *The Hero With a Thousand Faces*, originally published in 1949, his theories have enchanted legions of devoted followers and fanned the flames of detractors. Though Campbell remains popular outside of the academy, numerous scholars in the realms of Comparative Mythology have been critical of his writings (Lundwall, 2006). Campbell's work has been described as elitist (Segal, 1992, p.42) and culturally imperialistic (Oldmeadow, 2004, p.111), and folklorist Alan Dundes writes of Campbell, 'there is no single idea promulgated by amateurs that has done more harm to serious folklore study than the notion of archetype (2005, p.397). Feminist critics have also found fault in Campbell's male-centric heroic monomyth, noting that Campbell's 'archetypal female is essentially passive' (Lefkowits, 1990, p.432).

Even if Campbell's reputation has suffered slings and arrows at the hands of folklorists and mythologists, his theories continue to influence storytellers and filmmakers. George Lucas famously acknowledged how Campbell's dissection of the hero's journey influenced the Star Wars trilogy, and Christopher Vogler turned Campbell's monomyth into a 'practical guide' for screenwriters in his book *The Writer's Journey*.

What exactly is this monomyth and why has it become such a lightning rod for both devotion and controversy? As Campbell explains,

> A hero ventures forth from the world of common day into a region of supernatural wonder: fabulous forces are there encountered and a decisive victory is won: the hero comes back from this mysterious adventure with the power to bestow boons on his fellow man. (Campbell, 1971, p.30)

Campbell claims that all mythologies from every culture across the world, spanning all time periods, ultimately have a common narrative—the story of the hero's journey:

> The mythological hero … is lured, carried away, or else voluntarily proceeds, to the threshold of adventure. There he encounters a shadow presence that guards the passage. The hero may defeat or conciliate this power and go alive into the kingdom of the dark … Beyond the threshold, then, the hero journeys through a world of unfamiliar yet strangely intimate forces, some of which severely threaten him (test), some of which give magical aid (helpers). When he arrives at the nadir of the mythological round, he undergoes a supreme ordeal and gains his reward. The final work is that of the return … The boon that he brings restores the world. (pp.245-6)

In his book *The Writer's Journey*, Christopher Vogler adapts Campbell's monomyth for the three-act structure of narrative storytelling. Vogler summarizes:

The hero is introduced in his ORDINARY WORLD where he receives the CALL TO ADVENTURE. He is RELUCTANT at first to CROSS THE FIRST THRESHOLD where he eventually encounters TESTS, ALLIES and ENEMIES. He reaches the INNERMOST CAVE where he endures the SUPREME ORDEAL. He SEIZES THE SWORD or the treasure and is pursued on the ROAD BACK to his world. He is RESURRECTED and transformed by his experience. He RETURNS to his ordinary world with a treasure, boon, or ELIXIR to benefit his world (Vogler, 1998, p.26).[1]

Since Vogler examines this mythic structure from the perspective of storytellers, specifically filmmakers and screenwriters, he is also using this same journey motif to explain the character arc of the hero's internal journey (Vogler, 213).

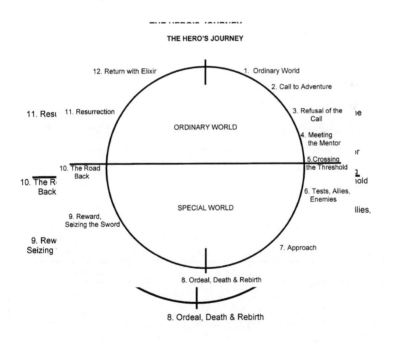

THE HERO'S JOURNEY

---

[1] On the "Hero's Journey" page of his accompanying website The Writer's Journey, www.thewritersjourey.com, Vogler has additionally adapted Maureen Murdock's *Heroine's Journey* to address issues of gender bias that have been leveled against Campbell's monomyth.

THE HERO'S INNER JOURNEY

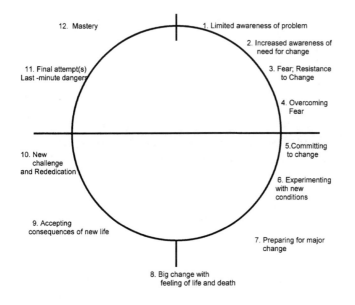

Illustrations from Vogler, www.thewritersjourney.com

Christopher Vogler "The Hero's Journey"

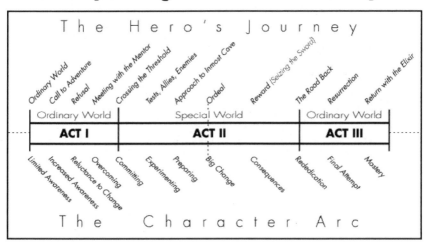

Illustration from Huntly, 2007, based on Vogler, 1998.

To accompany the archetypal hero on his journey, Vogler also identifies archetypal characters that typically show up along the path of the hero's journey, including the mentor, the threshold guardian, the herald, the shapeshifter, the shadow, and the trickster (Vogler, 1998, p.32), many of whom can also often be found along the path of the information quest.

From the Hero's Quest to the Information Quest

As Vogler observes,

> The values of the Hero's Journey are what's important. The images of the basic version – young heroes seeking magic swords from old wizards, maidens risking death to save loved ones, knights riding off to fight evil dragons in deep caves, and so on – are just symbols of universal life experiences. The symbols can be changed infinitely to suit the story at hand and the needs of the society. The Hero's Journey is easily translated … by substituting modern equivalents for the symbolic figures and props of the hero's story … Modern heroes may not be going into caves and labyrinths to fight mythical beasts, but they do enter a Special World and an Inmost Cave … The Hero's Journey is infinitely flexible, capable of endless variation without sacrificing any of its magic, and will outlive us all. (1998, pp.26-7)

If we take this assertion a step further, not only can we see the hero's journey in the stories that are told through various media, from books to movies to comics, but we can see the hero's journey in almost any quest, including the information-seeking quest. If we assume our information-seeker to be a college student new to scholarly research, we might be able to chart her course along the following path of the hero's journey:

1. She inhabits her ORDINARY WORLD where she typically seeks information from known resources to which she was introduced in high school or has discovered on the Internet.

2. The HERALD, her instructor, issues a CALL TO ADVENTURE in the form of a college-level assignment that requires scholarly research.

3. She is RELUCTANT at first or REFUSES THE CALL to enhance her information-seeking behaviors, assuming that she can find what she needs without additional training in finding and using scholarly resources.

4. After encouragement from MENTORS, such as instructors, librarians, and advisors, she eventually realizes she won't be able to produce quality work without getting some training and assistance in library research.

5. She must CROSS THE FIRST THRESHOLD by entering the SPECIAL WORLD where she can access scholarly academic research. In the university setting, this first threshold might be seeking help from a librarian, learning where to access resources, learning how to find her way around the library system and where to find databases, and learning how to get into these databases, such as through use of a campus proxy server or Virtual Private Network.

6. She encounters TESTS, ALLIES, AND ENEMIES along her path. Her ENEMIES might include the research resources that lead her down the wrong paths, such as the TRICKSTER (hoax), the SHAPESHIFTER (crowd-sourced), and the SHADOW (biased) – Internet sites that prove unreliable as resources for her scholarly research. In addition to MENTORS (librarians and instructors), her ALLIES might be research guides or tools and resources to help her flesh out her topic and find appropriate resources. Her TESTS might involve learning information literacy skills that teach her to utilize the library databases effectively and efficiently and how to evaluate and use the resources she discovers.

7. She crosses the second Threshold and APPROACHES THE INMOST CAVE. Guided by her librarian MENTOR, she has acquired the skills and tools necessary to enter the belly of the beast and find and evaluate reliable research resources needed for her scholarship. She has also learned how to utilize the research resources ethically and responsibly and has gained tools and tips for avoiding plagiarism and now knows how to incorporate research into her writing using appropriate citation formats.

8. Once inside the INMOST CAVE, she endures the ORDEAL by using her research for her writing assignment and completing her paper.

9. Her REWARD comes in the form of a good grade.

10. She pursues THE ROAD BACK by celebrating her reward.

11. She crosses the third Threshold by experiencing a transformative RESURRECTION, which is the realization that her reward was not only the good grade achieved on this one assignment, but was in fact the lessons and skills acquired along the path that will aid her in her next information quest.

12. She RETURNS WITH THE ELIXIR, which involves bringing her enhanced research skills to aid her in other classes and to aid her in her post-undergraduate pursuits. She found the Holy Grail of her information quest – the skills and knowledge needed to become a lifelong learner.

We can see how the arc of Vogler's character growth also fits this model of the hero's journey:

1. Our college student has a LIMITED AWARNESS OF A PROBLEM. She is unaware that her limited research skills are inadequate for college-level work or for producing scholarship within a chosen discipline.

2. She gains an INCREASED AWARENESS from her instructor about the need to find and use scholarly academic resources in her research.

3. She initially has a RELUCTANCE TO CHANGE and tries to find resources on her own.

4. She OVERCOMES her RELUCTANCE TO CHANGE and recognizes she needs help.

5. She COMMITS TO CHANGE by seeking assistance from a librarian, attending research workshops, and seeking out resources and tools that help expand and enhance her research and information literacy skills.

6. She EXPERIMENTS WITH FIRST CHANGE by attempting to use the databases, tools, and skills to which she has been introduced.

7. She PREPARES FOR BIG CHANGE by gathering her research resources.

8. She ATTEMPTS BIG CHANGE by critically evaluating her research and incorporating her research into her paper.

9. The CONSEQUENCES OF THE ATTEMPT are apparent in the improvements she has demonstrated in her research and writing.

10. She REDEDICATES TO CHANGE by recognizing that the research skills she used on this paper helped her achieve a better grade.

11. Her FINAL ATTEMPT AT BIG CHANGE is using her newfound information literacy skills for a new challenge in another class.

12. Her FINAL MASTERY OF THE PROBLEM is an enhanced understanding that she has added valuable skills to her arsenal and knows how to approach and conquer information challenges and knows where to get additional help when needed.

Meet Sir Learnsalot and the Sorceress Librarian

With an understanding of the information quest as a type of hero's journey, I set out to further demonstrate this connection through a series of tutorials called 'The Tales of Sir Learnsalot and the Sorceress Librarian.' My goal was to create a character who was himself on an information quest, and I decided to give the story a narrative arc so that students could follow along, and learn as the character learns. As a solo librarian in a departmental reading room that is administered by an academic department but affiliated with the larger university library system, my primary focus was to aid students who are using our departmental facility, the Grace M. Hunt Memorial English Reading Room.

To add a bit of whimsy and levity into the tutorials, I created an animated protagonist, and since I'm a librarian in an English Department collection, I wanted to incorporate a discipline-related theme. Thus I created the animated character Sir Learnsalot.

I structured the video tutorials along the path of the hero's quest: Separation, Initiation/Transformation, and the Return, assigning each video a set of learning outcomes that correspond to the hero's course along this discipline-focused information literacy journey. Each video includes a fantasy sequence that serves as a metaphor for the learning objective of the module, followed by a consultation session between Sir Learnsalot and the librarian, with screencast demonstrations intercut into the conversation. The individual videos can be found on the Grace M. Hunt Memorial English Reading Room YouTube channel (http://innovativelibraries.org.uk/RR):

- The Tale of Sir Learnsalot and the Sorceress Librarian

- Sir Learnsalot and the Library Labyrinth

- Sir Learnsalot and the Threshold Guardians: Keepers of the Proxy Server and Knights Who Say VPN

- Sir Learnsalot and the Compass of Research Strategy

- Three Rings to Rule Them All: Sir Learnsalot and the Test of Boolean Logic

- Sir Learnsalot and the Tricksters & Shapeshifters of the Internet

- Sir Learnsalot and the Search Through Catalogus Librorum

- Sir Learnsalot and the Journey Through the Sea of Journals

- Sir Learnsalot and the Community of Guides

The videos have also been mapped onto the graphic representation of the Hero's Journey on the following Prezi presentation:

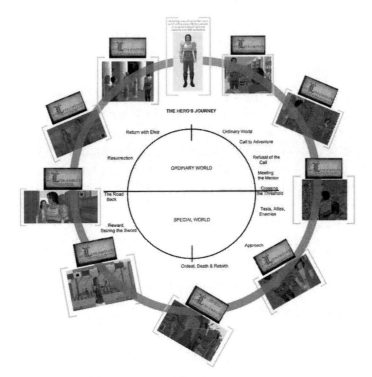

http://innovativelibraries.org.uk/SirPrezi

The first video, Sir Learnsalot and the Sorceress Librarian, demonstrates the hero's CALL TO ADVENTURE. At first, he is RELUCTANT to accept help in narrowing and focusing his research topic, but after encouragement from the librarian MENTOR, he sets upon the path of learning how to more efficiently and effectively conduct library research. By accepting help from his supernatural aid, the Sorceress Librarian, in Sir Learnsalot and the Library Labyrinth he discovers how to find information about the larger library system in general and the English Reading Room in particular and embarks upon his journey.

In Sir Learnsalot and the Threshold Guardians, he CROSSES THE FIRST THRESHOLD by learning how to use the VPN client to access library-licensed content. In Sir Learnaslot and the Compass of Research Strategy, he has now crossed over into the SPECIAL WORLD where he must chart his course towards finding, evaluating, and using discipline-focused library resources. He is TESTED along the path, and in Sir Learnsalot and the Test of Boolean Logic, he must pass the initiation challenge by mastering basic information literacy skills, such as using keywords to search library databases. He also must learn to recognize and defeat ENEMIES such as TRICKSTERS, SHAPESHIFTERS, and SHADOWS, which can correspond to non-reliable resources and Internet sites. In Sir Learnsalot and the Tricksters and Shapeshifters of the Internet, he adds to his arsenal by learning to use the CRAAP evaluation. He is now ready to APPROACH THE INMOST CAVE by learning to use the library catalog in Sir Learnsalot and the Search Through Catalogus Librorum.

Once inside the INMOST CAVE, he delves even deeper in Sir Learnsalot and the Journey Through the Sea of Journals, where he learns how to find peer-reviewed scholarly journal articles for his research. He has succeeded in his REVELATION, TRANSFORMATION, and ATONEMENT – he now knows where to find and how to use discipline-focused library resources, and he has the information literacy skills necessary to embark upon future information quests.

Though his supernatural guide, the Sorceress Librarian, has accompanied him this far down the path, there are parts of the journey he will travel alone, or he will need to also seek other helpers along his path towards his REWARD and the ROAD BACK.

He RETURNS triumphant from his quest with the skills necessary to not only produce scholarship in his chosen discipline, but also armed with the knowledge of where to get more help and how to be successful in his next information quest.

From Quest to Game

The next logical step might be to envision the information quest as an adventure game. In the seminal work, *What Video Games Have to Teach Us About Learning and Literacy*, Gee (2007) demonstrates how games can parallel information-seeking behaviors and foster learning. Many recent scholars have noted the similarities between gaming and the research process, examining how 'games present the same mythic challenges as Campbell's metamyth' (Smale, 2011, p.48) and how 'games appropriate the monomythic folkloric kingdom creating a postmodern rechanneling of traditional content elements and structures (Sherman, 2013, p.256). Dickey (2006) examines how 'the common structure found in most adventure games ... is the quest' (p.254), and he maps a similar learning quest to Vogler's interpretation of the hero's journey (p.255-6).

Thus, I wanted to turn the Sir Learnsalot series into a game. Using the video gamification platform ParWinr, I added some gaming elements to the videos and embedded these into Sir Learnsalot's mock blog post, The Adventures of Sir Learnsalot (http://adventuresofsirlearnsalot.blogspot.com/), where questions and challenges have been added to the videos, allowing the student watcher to play along and earn the prize at the end of the series of video modules, conference of the title 'Knight of the English Reading Room.'

http://adventuresofsirlearnsalot.blogspot.com/p/sir-learnsalot-and-sorceress-librarian.html

Sir Learnsalot and the Sorceress Librarian

Conclusion

Whether the information need is small or epic, each information-seeking adventure can be like the hero's quest – heeding the call of the herald, seeking help and guidance from mentors, gathering tools for the journey, mapping out a course, embarking upon the journey, facing challenges and trials, and venturing deep into the darkness of the cave to emerge victorious and return home triumphant. Indeed, the information-seeking process in its entirety can be mapped to the hero's journey of Joseph Campbell's monomyth and the quest narrative. Thus, turning the learning process into a quest narrative and quest game can be a fun way to introduce students to the information literacy skills that will serve them well in their own information journeys.

References

Adams, M. V. (2008). Does myth (still) have a function in Jungian studies? Modernity, metaphor, and psycho-mythology. In L. Huskinson, (Ed.). Dreaming the myth onwards: New directions in Jungian therapy and thought (pp. 81-90). New York: Routledge.

Campbell, J. (1971). The hero with a thousand faces (2d ed.). Princeton, N. J.: Princeton University Press.

Dickey, M. D. (2006). Game design narrative for learning: Appropriating adventure game design narrative devices and techniques for the design of interactive learning environments. Educational Technology Research and Development, 54(3), 245–263. doi:10.1007/s11423-006-8806-y

Dundes, A. (2005). Folkloristics in the Twenty-First Century (AFS Invited Presidential Plenary Address, 2004). Journal of American Folklore, 118, 470, 385-408.

Gee, J. P. (2007). What video games have to teach us about learning and literacy. New York: Palgrave Macmillan.

Harris, A., & Rice, S. E. (2008). Gaming in academic libraries: collections, marketing, and information literacy. Chicago: Association of College and Research Libraries.

Harris, R. (2012). Hero's Journey: Life's Great Adventure. The hero's journey: Life's great adventure. Retrieved from http://www.yourheroicjourney.com/heros-journey-lifes-great-adventure/

Harris, R., & Thompson, S. (1997). The hero's journey: A guide to literature and life. Napa, CA: Ariane Publications.

Huntly, C. (2007). How and why Dramatica is different from six other story paradigms. Dramatica Story Theory. Retrieved from http://dramatica.com/articles/how-and-why-dramatica-is-different-from-six-other-story-paradigms

Labre, M. P., & Duke, L. (2004). 'Nothing like a brisk walk and a spot of demon slaughter to make a girl's night': The construction of the female hero in the Buffy Video Game. Journal of Communication Inquiry, 28(2), 138–156. doi:10.1177/0196859903261795

Lefkowitz, M. R. (1990). Mythology: The myth of Joseph Campbell. The American Scholar, 59(3), 429–434. doi:10.2307/41211815

Lundwall, J. K. (2006). Reinvigorating innovation: Theory, myth, and the Campbell critics. Cosmos and Logos: Cosmology, Mythology and Ancient Mysteries. Retrieved from http://www.cosmosandlogos.com/category/000081.php

Murdock, M. (1990). The heroine's journey (1st ed.). Boston, Mass. : [New York, N.Y.]: Shambhala ; Distributed in the U.S. by Random House.

Oldmeadow, H. (2004). Journeys East: 20th century Western encounters with Eastern religious traditions. Bloomington, Ind: World Wisdom.

Segal, R. (1992). Myths versus religion for Campbell. In K. L. Golden (Ed.), Uses of comparative mythology: Essays on the work of Joseph Campbell (pp. 39-51). New York: Garland Pub.

Shearer, A. (2004). On the making of myths: Mythology in training. Journal of Jungian Theory and Practice, 6(2), 1-13.

Sherman, S. R. (1997). Perils of the princess: Gender and genre in video games. Western Folklore, 56(3/4), 243–258. doi:10.2307/1500277

Smale, M. A. (2011). Learning through quests and contests: Games in information literacy instruction. Journal of Library Innovation, 2(2), 36–55.

Vogler, C. (n.d.). Hero's journey. Retrieved from http://www.thewritersjourney.com/hero%27s_journey.htm

Vogler, C. (1998). The writer's journey: mythic structure for writers. Studio City, CA: M. Wiese Productions.

Exploring information landscapes and bubbles: facilitating students' discovery of their information selves /
Andy Burkhardt and Alan Carbery

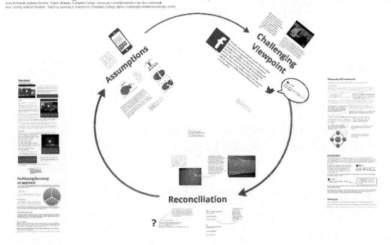

This chapter is in the form of a Prezi at
http://innovativelibraries.org.uk/ExpPrezi

Abstract

At Champlain College Library, our information literacy programme is not just about teaching students how to search library databases, or find scholarly articles; it's about engaging students in critical conversations about their information choices as information consumers. This chapter will narrate how we engage first year students in these conversations using multiple methods, tools, and learning objects.

Through the use of mobile phone polling and a TED Talk about filter bubbles, we facilitate student discovery of a wider information landscape. This, in turn, leads to inquiry into corporate and external influences on information as well as a questioning of the implications of personal information choices. Students discover how they both use and *are used by* information. This leads students to think of their information world in new and thought-provoking ways.

By engaging students in these meaningful and contextualized conversations, we open our students up to transformative learning moments (Mezirow, 1997) that help then rediscover their information selves.

References:

Mezirow, J. (1997) Transformative learning: theory to practice, *New Directions for Adult and Continuing Education*, (74), pp. 5-12.

Pariser, E. (2011) *Beware online "filter bubbles"* [video] http://www.ted.com/talks/eli_pariser_beware_online_filter_bubbles.ht ml [Accessed 25 February 2013].

Journeying without a map leads to … adventures or accidents? A study of drama academics' approaches to discovering information / Zoë Johnson and Andrew Walsh

(photo by Zoë Johnson)

Our starting point

This chapter uses the voices of twelve drama lecturers and researchers to tell stories about their experiences of information literacy. It is based on a series of semi-structured interviews covering different aspects of information literacy. Although we gave participants a definition of information literacy (in this case the JISC iSKills definition below), we also gave them considerable freedom to discuss issues arising and to go off on tangents they felt were worth exploring.

"The ability to identify, assess, retrieve, evaluate, adapt, organise and communicate information within an iterative context of review and reflection." JISC iSkills definition (2005).

We approached our research in the belief that definitions such as the one we've selected tell only part of the story. "Information literacy" often gets reduced to checklists of skills or competencies that someone must demonstrate to be classed as "information literate", which we feel misses the point. We've taken a more experiential approach to the idea of information literacy in this research: we believe that information literacy looks different depending on the context it occurs in. It always deals with identifying; assessing; retrieving; evaluating; adapting; organising and communicating information ... but this looks different depending on what you are trying to achieve. So, these elements change when we book a holiday (and need to decide where to go; how to find out the best deals; the nicest places to stay in our price range; etc.); or carry out research within drama, like our academics; or put together an exhibition ... they alter depending on the environment in which we work.

In this approach we are heavily influenced by Christine Bruce (Seven Faces of Information Literacy, 1997) and by later research discussing "relational" information literacy. We also anticipated that each of our interviewees would bring their own experience and apply that to the context in which they operate, so we would see different but equally valid ways of being "information literate", with different routes through the information forest but arriving at the same destination in the end.

We were interested in how drama researchers and lecturers experienced information literacy. How did they act when searching for information? How did they organise, use and evaluate that information for their teaching or research? What lessons could we take from their narratives to help students become information literate within this context?

Our research elicited several different themes which we have grouped into two main approaches, described in the words of the interviewees themselves. These show how the interviewees have been successful (or not) in navigating the information forest, and the nature of the influences that shaped our interviewees' information literacy journeys.

We then outline how we as librarians could use this information to help us lay trails through the forest for students to follow. Hopefully these will prove to be useful, stone trails the students can build upon and re-use, rather than breadcrumbs prone to disappearing before they can guide the students to their desired destinations.

The group of drama academics interviewed covers a range of backgrounds and specialist areas as well as being of mixed age and experience. Their varying experiences in academia, both as student and as teacher, influenced how they approached their information journey. Their subject focus, whether highly theoretical and conceptual and delivered through lectures and seminars, or practical and improvisational in studios, again shaped their attitude towards engaging with information.

Despite the diversity of experiences and approaches among our participants, two clear routes into the forest emerged. We've described these as "Following the paths" and "Exploring the landscape". These routes aren't mutually exclusive and there was considerable overlap, but our interviewees tended towards one approach or the other.

Following the paths

The nature of information literacy in this grouping had certain characteristics:

- A core or safe knowledge base
- A need to fill the gaps
- They look for direct quotes or exact connections
- They "experience" then read
- Often vague ideas of what you "should have" leads to a convoluted journey to a desired destination

This approach is characterised by a feeling of "I know what I am looking for, just might not be sure of the exact location", which built on participants' experience, their subject knowledge, their previous reading or information gathering. Some referred to it as "boxes" or "concepts" with which to approach information, a context in which to search so they knew what waymarkers to look out for.

Participants in this group already knew the language to use and the practitioners or scholars they wanted to read.

> *I tend to start from what I know. I probably use my personal library at home as an extended memory bank. If I haven't got the knowledge, I might just go and sort of scout around a little bit, in order to develop my thinking.*

This was a common concept - using the experience which had been gained by having studied for an extended period. This developed into a core knowledge that they tried to find ways of passing on as a safe base for students.

> *It would be knowledge that I have, and then I need to check that I was kind of thinking of it in specific places or hoping that the students can access it from specific places. So it might be in my head thinking, oh, that book's really useful but I'll go and check that it is as useful as I thought.*

In order to pass this core knowledge on, participants in this group were thinking constantly that they need to reference and signpost it clearly for students. They needed to give a reliable route in for their students.

> *I tend to turn to the names that I know first of all, and go back to those readers and look at what they've already got in there and what they also reference. So I start to go from academics that I know and have some synergy with and faith in, and turn to who they are. So I go by reputation of those things.*

A lot of the interviewees admitted to being experts in a small research field, but also were keen to point out that as teachers they could not retain all the information and needed to point out the key authors or practitioners. Some taught very close to their research area, while others explored the "current topic", e.g. current trends in applied theatre, or contemporary writing for the theatre.

This changed their approach, as they were either refreshing their knowledge or opening up new avenues and looking for ways to extend the knowledge they class as reliable in order to pass it onto students.

> *... the choices that I make are pedagogically driven rather than creatively driven. It's not a vehicle for me to explore my own aesthetic interest ... I'd love to work on that show. The measurements have got to be - is it appropriate for first year, second years, third years? Why? What are they gaining from what they're learning? How does it balance with the other possibilities they're being offered at that point? Those are the choices being made rather than an enthusiasm for the piece itself really. I personally don't sit and watch a piece and say, God, I'd love to do that with it, and then try and find a way of making that happen. I tend to think, is this appropriate? And if it is, then work out what I need to research to teach that piece of work. Because it may be a piece of work that I don't have much interest in or is not something that is naturally something that I would direct or lead, but I can see its value and I can see why that would be useful for students. So I'm going to have to learn it.*

> *I tend to use reading for students ... if it's books, to go - you need to do some independent study on this; and not tell them which bits to read, which bits are directly relevant, because it's about widening knowledge and trying to get them to surprise me with something that they've uncovered; rather than knowing exactly what they've read and learnt and assimilated.*

This group was often torn between recommending restricted guided reading (some gave specific handouts, some summarised key messages) and vaguer pointers towards theorists to encourage creativity. This often changed according to year group, with first-year students having their hands held at the start of their research journeys, and later released "into the wild" by the end of their second year or the beginning of their final year.

> *Let's just get the basics under their belts and the classics under their belts, if you like, of what they need to know; what's safe and steady*

for those levels. So I tend to work within what I would know for first year...

There was evidence at times of a clash between academics who want students to become independent straight away and others who wanted to ease their transition more gradually.

> *... our students tend to be very, very 'practical approach' so it really is, "think of this and actually do it, try it. Now go back and evaluate and analyse your own work or evaluate and analyse those of others". That's where I ask them to, "okay, go and find something which is going to back up your work and textualise your work", and that's where I might send them to papers or quotes or whatever.*

This reflects our own experience of how many students work. However, they often struggle to back up their practical work in the way the above quote suggests. They have not learnt the language of the field, and therefore cannot search for themselves independently. Instead they often require the connections to be made more obvious: e.g. read this book and you will clearly see the correlation with your practical work.

Interviewees who fell into this group often showed a desire to stay with the safe set of material they know in their field.

> *I'm not very catholic in my tastes, I don't, I don't read widely in theatre at all. I stay very much within the field of my interest and teaching. I read widely like in the rest of culture, but not in theatre.*

When discussing how they saw and/or expected students to approach the research process, this group felt that first years needed to be taught the "boxes", shown the paths, guided through the wealth of information whilst being encouraged to question and look for what interested, excited or just plain "spoke" to them. This approach took the form of quite a lot of targeted reading either through set weekly readings or simplified summaries of the concepts.

So I have to pick apart what all the theorists are saying and then unpick it again so that I can put it together to give to the first years. Because first years in theory have trouble. That their head ... the gears aren't meshing yet.

They felt a strong need to give students some guidance as to where they are going in a language in which they understand.

They have to structure, they have to have understanding, they have to basic building blocks and they need to know where to find that and they need to be pointed towards it and they have to be told that it's important. As well as finding out for themselves that it's important. They also need to go off-piste and then that's when they're really soaring, bringing back all of that stuff they've found themselves, all these connections they've made themselves and apply that on top of those building blocks of knowledge then they're really beginning to soar.

So only once they had the core knowledge could they be trusted to go off the beaten path ...

[Students] don't have the conceptual categories, so I think it goes right over their head. They don't know what to do with it, they know they enjoyed it, and maybe they know that "wow, that surprised me!" and in conversation, you can push them a little bit more to "what did you think happened there?" But they don't have any boxes to put that in, so I sometimes sort of, I try to, when I'm working with students, I try to find some ways in at the very outset, to establish some boxes that they can start to gather experiences into. And that seems like a similar sort of thing, is how are they going to know what's important, how are they going to know it when they see it?
'Cos otherwise, if I went into the rainforest, and there's all these...I'd just go "oh, look at all these great animals" I wouldn't come up with anything, I wouldn't know what to do with that. I think it's like that for them. And then I think, it's about priming them sufficiently without trying to put some sort of theoretical thing before they have the experience 'cos I wouldn't want to be told I had to learn categories

of bird type before I went and had a good time in the rainforest but, at the same time, if I wanted to come out of it with some knowledge or some retained information about the birds, I think I would need something to enable me to see what I was looking at.

And the hope is to encourage them to hold those conceptual "boxes", as I am calling them, so that when something happens, they know where to put it, they know what it relates to and then you would hope, that then when they go to the literature or whatever else that they can make those connections. Some of it because it's obvious, "concentration we've going on about" and I can look up concentration in the index but I also have to go with them, [thumping the table to emphasise] "nobody is going to have, there's no book in the library called whatever this thing is" so what are the component parts you might look for? And speak to them quite directly about how are you going to recognise this when you see it, 'cos they're not going to do that for you, they're not going to tell you, Grotowski's not going to give you any sentences with the words "devising" in them! So how are you going to see where he's going to speak to your experience?

This grouping sometimes found searching for information frustrating, as they were looking for things they felt should be there. Their mental model was predicated on gaps in subject material or students' knowledge , so their time was spent searching for what they felt was the exact information needed to fill those gaps.

Exploring the landscape

Participants who fell into the second group demonstrated a genuine enjoyment of exploring information, being open to what might be out there, continually seeking out new paths and alternative views, and taking risks.

The characteristics of this grouping were:

- Continually taking in information
- Storing of random ideas and making connections later

- They want to read and experience simultaneously
- Knowing what you have leads to quick and rewarding journey

Instead of maintaining a safe set of material these participants looked for new connections between practice and the material they encountered.

> *I like the browsing experience, and I'm a very whimsical person, I'm not a methodical person. I'm very much a kind of "what grabs me" kind of person ... so with periodicals, I like flicking through them, have a glance at the editorial ... titles ... little abstracts ... look at the pictures.*

Apart from time limitations (this activity often is saved for the summer months in our interviewees), this seemed a common approach by staff but we feel it is rarely seen in students, until perhaps 3rd year when they start larger independent research and start to get excited about choosing "their own" topic to explore.

> *I generally have a sense that there's something I don't know and I try to work out how go and find out about it. Usually it's that way, but sometimes I trip over something or some practitioner and I go "oh that's interesting" and I pursue things that way. [...] I like research as a creative stimulus. If you find out what somebody did it makes you go "oh great, cool, I'm not going to do that BUT, I'll tell you what THAT'S really interesting" and I can go off on my own journeys with things.*

The use of the word "journey" is of particular interest here, and in fact this was a recurring metaphor used by these participants. They expressed themselves in terms of the journey being more important than the destination. They looked for things that interested them and would set them off on a voyage of discovery.

> *Again, it's just a matter of what captures your interest. Sometimes I need an idea. Like I'm beginning to think now about stuff that I might want to direct next year, or modules that I might want to teach, and so it's just a change in mindset kind of going: what can I be receptive*

to? So, I might go to the newspapers a bit more often; or from January on if I've got time I might make more of an effort to go and see shows; and if I can I'll read a bit more fiction or whatever. So, those sorts of things just to kind of open up – have the radio on more consciously – those sorts of things, so that when I have to make a decision about offering a particular show or something I can think: yes, I'd like to do that. But there's sort of a long gestation period sometimes. It's about a freshening up and being open to the accidental thing or the thing you don't know about, which is actually really great.

They liked to take a serendipitous approach, allowing for exploration around the information forest, a kind of meandering without necessary purpose.

That stimulus to teaching, it makes me think, it kind of opens doors, it lets me mull and muse and stare out the window and wonder, and then go "ah, I wonder if I could try this" but I never use research directly, pedagogically. [...] I'm really interested in research as a way of entering into the minds of people who came before me as a stimulus, in the same way I read a novel or a look at a painting or watch a cow eat grass. It's all a stimulus to possibilities.

In initial stages of creativity it's really good to be out of your comfort zone or to be in unfamiliar circumstances and surroundings because that's where new connections start to happen. So actually that chaos and uncertainty is a really good place for them to be when they first approach a subject. Although it doesn't feel necessarily safe place to be, it's a very useful place to be.

So we're taught to be very observant of everything. Because you never know when you can use it. So for me it's like ... you know, "Think about this", or, "Look at that". And so that's really what's fuelled me in terms of this ... I don't think I can even call it a need any more, because it's just so much a part of me. It just is. I'm always observing and just taking little bits on board. And it all becomes the information that feeds into everything I do. My students ask me, "How do you know so much?" Well because I pay attention. I'm curious. And so that's really what's probably driven all that.

Some interviewees actively encouraged this curiosity in their students, particularly those who focused on practical teaching. These participants wanted the students to "experience" the acting approach or the technique, or to "have a play" with the piece of technical apparatus *before* researching or reading about it.

Others simply embraced the randomness in which information may come at you in everyday life – seeping themselves in culture, whether literature, television, film or music, and being open to something of interest, of use, whether now or later. They were continually curious and receptive to new ideas or pathways that could lead them to another piece of research or a new avenue for teaching.

There are benefits to having a map (or box of concepts), as used heavily by the *following the paths* group, in a creative subject such as Drama; however, there is also great appeal in the natural, impulsive discovery of a new idea or pathway, before having to dissect it into its academic parts.

> *Because in the end the only reason I'm interested in research is that I can go into the space and deal with indefinable things. Because performance is indefinable. So I am looking to arm myself with the ability to sculpt unexpected moments with a performer. And all of the research is just for that.*

When these interviewees talked about what this approach meant for students, they referred to workshops and practical sessions as the safe place to play with ideas and feelings and experiences. They help students make connections with the academic information, to start recognising the language to use to explain the emotional response. They wanted to turn a raw experience into a reflective piece of work, set in an academic context. They wanted to get students to be excited about the possibility of random connections, to stay aware of their surroundings and how other media might influence their work.

> *But normally I think it is about supplementing their [students'] experiential knowledge with the reading in the practice based modules. Because I don't do the lecture seminars on the whole, I can come from this practice base and go, "Let's get you learning. And*

then in order to get you thinking and writing and analysing what you're learning and putting this experience into the wider field this is where you need to start reading and thinking". So, it kind of works that way. My shorthand is, "Let's do some stuff". ((Laughs)) I say to them, "We're going to start by doing some stuff. And then we'll start talking about it".

And so ... because I'm not planning out how each moment is going to go in that ... in that room. Because so much of it is determined by what they do. I don't want to get locked into something and them miss a discovery. Because I said, "Well, no we have to do this now". Because acting isn't an A, B, C thing. It isn't linear. Performance is not something that you ... if you do X, Y and Z you will not be a performer. It can't happen that way. You go ... you don't know what's going to inspire the kid to finally make that leap. And so I want it to be as open as possible for them to make the discoveries. And for me to make discoveries. I've learned so much watching these kids. It's like "Wow! That was really cool! Do you have any idea what you just did?" and they're like, "Nope". "Let me explain ..." and so that's ... that's how I ... that's how I work practically.

Where these academics focussed on the importance of experiencing something before reading the theory, it was seen as making the reading much more relevant and pertinent. The reading couldn't be set beforehand as they couldn't pre-define the core, important, safe texts: they needed to emerge from making sense of the practice.

This group of interviewees often had a more joyful and playful approach to being information literate. They took the material they read and applied it to their practice, rather than feeling the need to constantly fill in gaps. Their information journey was therefore often shorter and more rewarding for them. It didn't need to be sought out for a specific reason or need, but instead could form part of their richer academic life and feed into their practice at a later date.

A key question for us, the authors as librarians, is how we get students to be as creative and playful in the library or on search engines as they are in the studio, workshop or rehearsal space?

Library staff can of course support both the approaches outlined above. They can enthuse and make the "Library" a safe place in which to play and experiment. Rather than getting bogged down with teaching the technology or the terminology of information systems, they can instead facilitate library users to explore the resources themselves. Once interested in a topic, there are few wrong answers - especially if students and staff can indicate the connections they've made. Being on hand, like a guide who lurks behind trees or appears at difficult forks in the path like a Cheshire cat on the branch, could also be a useful role for librarians to take, offering directions for those who need a set path and organisational skills for those that want to play and explore.

Getting to these approaches

How did our interviewees ended up with these approaches? How did they develop their own approaches to information literacy?

When we, the authors, did our first degrees, no material was online, information was seen as sparse rather than overwhelming, and we cannot remember receiving a library induction, let alone any information literacy skills teaching. We asked our interviewees how they "learnt" their information seeking and their research skills. Some could easily define how :

> *Q ...you said you sort of started in a family that was very information-seeking. Curious was the word, wasn't it? Has anyone ever taught you how to do this?*
>
> *R To be curious? Or how to ...?*
>
> *Q ... how to interact with information?*
>
> *R No. Not ... well ... yes, probably. I would say ... I would say that ... that my elementary and middle school education was really all about that. In that respect. I think they were just really subtle about it. [...] And so, using a library, and tracking down that information, now that I think about it, they were very sneaky. They had a project that was kind of an archaeology ... you were given clues, and you had to go find the book. And inside the book would be*

a clue. That you had to then use to find the next clue to find the next clue. And it was the story of … there were several stories that were all interlinked. But they were these documents. You were always looking for documents. And they had gone to the trouble of making it look like old parchment. And handwritten with ink and quill and all that stuff. It was amazing. And it taught us how to research. How different books tell you different things. And this was … was I 13? 12? I was hugely fortunate in terms of the education I received. Because that taught me how to look for things. How to explore. Totally forgot about that until today. That was really cool. God, that was a really fun project. It was something to do with the American Revolution, I think. But, you know, it was like diary entries. And … and … and little scraps of articles. And newspaper and things. And all the teachers … as far as I know, it was the Social Studies and the English teacher had created this all between the two of them. A huge, vast undertaking. And then the librarians were fine with it. They were … we were coming in and tearing apart the place trying to find things and going from book to book and asking them questions, and they knew, "Well …" and it was an amazing experience.

Perhaps getting students to consider their approaches and how they learn together with information specialists may help students learn information skills that work for them?

I think I followed a model that I followed for creative writing. […] I think I learnt that model at school through drama. How stories work really. And I'm kind of obsessed with story structure. […] So we talk about story and plot. I always think of story as all the information we've got about anything, the story is everything that we know about it and the plot then is how we arrange that information to tell the story, to give it some significance.

This interviewee taught the methodology of creative writing before becoming a drama academic, and he adapted this approach to all his academic creative outputs. His information literacy was framed by his experience of narrative structures.

This is personal history with libraries ... when I was very young,
maybe six, I don't know, my Dad took me and enrolled me into the
public library. I remember going in there all day when I was still at
primary school for a project and doing research. Finding out about
flora and fauna of Australasia or something. I'm not even sure if that
was the title but I learnt those words in the process of doing it and
looking in the reference library, kind of hunting things. So I learned
libraries, finding my way around libraries, at an early age. And I
regularly used libraries in my school, my grammar school, we did all
our private study periods in the library.

This relationship with using information and libraries again started to
be formed at an early age and was built upon during later studies.

The end of our journey and start of the next

Most interviewees just found themselves doing what felt natural or
right to them, without being aware of the origins of those feelings.
They often still questioned their expertise or efficiency in the process:

I don't think anyone has ever taught me anything [laughs] I think it's
just through doing it and responding to circumstance, given
circumstances. [...] So I think, it's just a case of using common sense
really, seeing what the task is and seeing how the students respond to
something, and seeing what is missing, what is it they need.

The question for librarians as educators is how to give enough
guidance and suggestions to students in finding the best way for them
to approach information literacy, whilst allowing them the freedom
and safe environment to explore and find their own methods.

My big thing is I want them to all develop their own approaches and
they have to have bespoke approaches to the research and have to find
out their own ways of doing it. And actually part of our job is to
deconstruct what they think and then help them reconstruct it.
Particularly in terms of the jump from A level into higher education

where they're increasingly taught how to pass things and how to display and regurgitate the right information. But that's a very different way of going about things than thinking and making your own connections between bits of material.

Going forward, we will be coding and analysing the interviews more formally to enable us to find ways of helping staff and students make sense of the information landscape and find their own ways through it. Whether they want to follow existing pathways or explore the landscape in a more freeform way, we hope to learn more about how librarians can support them in this continual process.

At work in the phenomenal field: can there be a person-centred library? / Nick Norton

> The educational structure which most effectively promotes significant learning is one in which 1) threat to the self of the learner is reduced to a minimum, and 2) differentiated perception of the field of experience is facilitated. (Rogers, 1951, p. 391)

I begin in a phenomenal field I call my own, a perceptual field; a field of experience. Now there is an awareness of the chair beneath, the pile of papers beside me, the sound of children in a school playground, a neighbour pounding something with a mallet. There is a growing hunger, a temptation to make lunch, at the same time an urgent pull to remain here, typing. Here, the computer below my hands. Yet this is not the field, not in its entirety, for the field unfolds and rolls all around. The sounds remind me of other sensations and memories; the memories bring forth associations, which in turn evoke meanings and comparisons. A narrative begins or, consciously brought to the present moment, I again begin. The closer the scrutiny the greater the scope of memory, meaning and association; even unto a bold assertion of unity. Each conscious state is 'to be phenomenally unified with each other' (Bayne, 2010, p. 31). If this is truly so large, do I have a right to call it my own?

Nonetheless, for practical purposes, this pragmatism of identity is where any investigation must begin. In time the pragmatism extends and fold back onto consciousness: this is understood as self.

... my hand, while it is felt from within, is also accessible from without, itself tangible ... it takes its place among the things it touches, is in a sense one of them, opens finally upon a tangible being of which it is also a part. Through this crisscrossing within it of the touching and the tangible, its own movements incorporate themselves into the universe they interrogate ... (Merleau-Ponty, 1968, p. 133)

We conceive of a self in the phenomena of our perception: our perception crosses over itself, so to speak, and seeks Self that conceives. It is the physicality of this which will be useful to us. Perception, consciousness, unity: each can be touted as abstractions yet we do not push and pull abstracts (except in painting); we speak them with tongue and mouth, we breathe through them. This embodied state is actual, as physical as the language with which I gasp the word: Coffee!

These words tapped out by clumsy fat fingers, these piles of paper I maintain in good order (for a moment): Information has not yet vanished into an immaterial realm of electricity (or ideology). Indeed, as ideas must be carried so the digital must also carry a body, must be a body of electron and of quantum. The library, therefore, it must be remembered, is a body. It is a memory and remembering; a perception and a perceiving. It is a collection and it is the collecting; a service and a servicing. The library is in our phenomenal field and of itself it holds forth its own phenomenal field because it is that which is perceived in the present moment (Syngg; Combs).

How can a library be said to be perceiving? In the main by the volition of the service it provides. That service is in itself of the multiple wills of the service providers. The service providers, the staff, are of course themselves persons; sensing, breathing, moving beings who encounter themselves and others, who in these encounters conceive of an identity, articulate that identity through their actions and receive it back via the perceiving the articulation of others.

There is great excitement in this. The persons. The collection. The exploration. When this is real, genuine - when there is congruence of person and service - in this sharing, diving after information, collaborating on projects, pooling knowledge, each is brightened through an awareness always open to the potent encounter, learning something new. The library is on the one hand presumed to be a stable entity, with its totality mapped by classification and subject; but the potential is such that this stability reveals an astonishing mutability. Map is not the territory: awareness linked through the phenomena of encounter makes learning, the wholly new and always possible.

This does not always pass as a fitting description of library, it must be said. How so? Bad hair day? Lack of coffee day? Incongruent, unreal, not genuine; persons maintain a persona in order to get by, and they do not enjoy what they perceive. Sometimes that lack of enjoyment is projected onto the collection or onto those who would try to engage in the contents of the collection. Sometimes the service users get caught in a set of mirrors so distorted that they, the users, are pre-emptively classified as 'problem'. This 'problem' is then given the energy of one's projected judgement (negativity), and becomes a persona. Persona grinds up again persona, the friction brings defensiveness. Hence there is, on occasion, a palpable sense that even before words the service provider can themselves be caught in perceptual crossfire and therefore become 'the problem'.

It is these unspoken conversations, or the barely sensed phenomena that get roughly bagged into rough categories, from which proceed impersonal dislikes and awkward social interactions. This sketched-out picture is one which typically hampers learning. Learning begins in that latent awareness which O'Neil and McMahon (2005) describe as 'readiness'; to be aware, to be ready, and to physically approach a body of information in this readiness, is to fairly guarantee a transformation of information into knowledge. Awareness is transmuted into learning; the learner may then be allowing their perceptual field to flow over into knowledge and this knowledge might be seen a culmination of previous inter-subjective conversations.

How can such unfolding of awareness into learning be hampered? If we return to the library, surely the collection is still there? The contents have not changed, our signage is clear, the reading lists are well catered for, why does that potent encounter not occur more often? Is it because our phenomenal field is too busy with persona? Our awareness is snagged on scripts (Berne), other issues fill our internal narratives (Ellis): *he hates me; what's she looking at; I'm not meant to be here; I don't get this; boring.* This the persona of the unhappy library user.

And what of the unhappy institution? Here they come again; same old questions, can't they read the signs? Look, I'm busy. They hate me.

What are they looking at? I'm not meant to be here; I don't get this (but I can't admit that); boring.

I will now describe a workplace on a register of fiction. This will allow me to conflate several conversations and stories; the workplace with all the unruly potential of an encounter in fable. In the skewed but powerful reality of fairy tale (Carter; Zipes) this becomes a *narrated* library rather than a *documented* library.

Milltown College is a mixed provision specialist art and design college, near buried in the wild growth of a busy metropolis. The mills have all been shut down and repurposed as shopping malls or urban dwelling spaces, the skyline bristles with towers built for civic ambition and to snare service sector wealth. It is a harsh environment for dreamers, and yet Milltown College has managed to nurture creative industry for over one hundred years. The student census has consistently returned over 90% satisfaction rates with the library. The library itself has dreamt; others also dream on its behalf, and these others do not often step amongst its collection. They rather dream of it as an object, a part of some greater machine.

Of course, should one continue in this register, eventually the story may end: My tale is done now, I can lie no more.

This unreliable narrator does have advantages, despite impishness. Objects are smuggled in beneath a subjective disguise. It is easier to have an emotional or subjective response to a singing teapot, or a teapot with a dormouse inside, than to endure a lecture on delirium and its ontological affect within the space-time continuum of childhood; likewise, there is less of an intellect-made chasm between 'truth objects' if they are simultaneously experienced as subjectively true.

Nonetheless it is chiasmic perception we are concerned with: the cross-over of phenomena in person-to-person encounter, not cross-dressing wolves and – hopefully – not the drama of an intrigue.

Milltown College as centre for visual study attracts a higher than average proportion of dyslexic students: roughly one-third of students on the FE courses, and a quarter in the larger intake of HE. These numbers fluctuate, of course; some enter post-compulsory education already knowing something about their learning difference, while others are identified during the course. A dyslexic diagnosis enables a greater degree of support to be given but is often an emotional event, a wholly new form of education being thrown into an already full schedule. The difference between FE and HE numbers may be in part because of the greater maturity of the HE intake. These students have developed their repertoire of coping mechanisms.

Dyslexia is present in an estimated one in ten of the general population. In conversations with A. and K. - staff who support learning differences - a few pertinent points came to the fore. Firstly, yes, students are intimidated: 'You're a scary man.' The librarian as ogre. But perhaps by the use of a magic potion called attentiveness we can become more charming? The library has supplemented the Dewey Decimal System with a colour coding division by subject matter: the dizziness of words and numbers can be somewhat allayed, therefore, if a student can be guided toward 'the red section'.

One should remember that general descriptions of dyslexia are only that, and that every learning difference is unique to each learner:

- Appears bright, highly intelligent, and articulate but unable to read, write, or spell at grade level.

- Labelled lazy, dumb, careless, immature, 'not trying hard enough,' or 'behaviour problem.'

- Isn't 'behind enough' or 'bad enough' to be helped in the school setting.

- High in IQ, yet may not test well academically; tests well orally, but not written.

- Feels dumb; has poor self-esteem; hides or covers up weaknesses with ingenious compensatory strategies; easily frustrated and emotional about school reading or testing.

- Talented in art, drama, music, sports, mechanics, story-telling, sales, business, designing, building, or engineering.

- Seems to 'Zone out' or daydream often; gets lost easily or loses track of time.

- Difficulty sustaining attention; seems 'hyper' or 'daydreamer.'

- Learns best through hands-on experience, demonstrations, experimentation, observation, and visual aids. (Davis, 1992, accessed May 2013.)

The daydreamer, the haptic learner, the attraction toward visual thinking: these are less symptoms and more like recruitment criteria. K. concurred that this theory of the match between dyslexia and visual thinking may be valid, but added that there is a further line of thought suggesting that visual education attracts learning differences because it is (falsely) perceived as less academic. When students discover there actually is required reading, and written work, then quite often a state of panic ensues. It is here that the interlaced talents of teaching staff, support staff and library must endeavour to weave an individual garment for each learner. K. insists that with the correct support (perhaps the garment is worn underneath the day apparel) dyslexia proves to be no barrier to academic success.

Under 2010 UK equality legislation all public institutions are required to take 'reasonable steps' to flexibly respond to disability. One approach to such adaption would be to make generic changes, 'best guesses' on what the next intake may present. There is, however, an inbuilt inefficiency in this approach. One cannot presume on individual learning styles in the same manner as one builds in wheelchair access. Cornell University, which runs a course in Person-Centered Planning, state that

> [p]erson-centered planning is a means for uncovering what is already there: the essence and extraordinary gifts and capacities of a person. […]

> Person-centered planning requires systems to respond in flexible and meaningful ways relative to the unique interests and needs of the focus person. (Cornell University Person-Centered Planning, accessed May, 2013)

Let's tell brief stories from library experience in each part of this journey. Let's pull together several worlds and see if this collaboration equals a new world or an uncomfortable fit or, perhaps, the beginning steps of another journey ...

I recall the librarian coming out and worrying over us, a small gang of gawking boys who have found the most horrific book possible: a catalogue of grotesquery, accident and mutilation. Bravado demanded sniggering and gasps of amazement (I felt sick but would not show it); the librarian fluttered: *No, no, now no. That is not at all what the book is for.* Thereafter the book retreated into the office, and bravado sufficient to asking for it never again appeared.

In the therapeutic model the manner of relating to a client has been statistically proven to be more important to the therapy's outcome than the practitioner's personal, demographic or professional characteristics. Positive outcomes are associated with a collaborative, caring, empathic and skilled way of relating (Cooper).

In conversation, N. and T. (professional counsellors in a post-compulsory educational setting) confirmed that this was true of their experience, and suggested to the library service that in order for a library user to feel committed to the process, a sense of equality, not paternalism, was required.

Of course it could be argued that in this memory of the school library the viewpoint is skewed. Was the book inappropriate for our age group; perhaps our sensationalism was ruining a carefully nurtured atmosphere of self-improvement? Similarly, the legal relationship between school staff and pupil is different to that of post-compulsory educational staff and their charges. Even so, a person-centred approach in services dealing directly with young people experiencing mental health and emotional problems (one in ten amongst children aged 5-16) does claim an overarching need to hear the young person's voice. Indeed, the approaches are to be 'derived from what young people say works' in services that are 'person-centred, holistic and inclusive' (*Listen Up!*).

A more recent study of 'the emotive topic' (McCluskey) of school behaviour repeatedly reports the children in compulsory education stressing the significance of 'fairness and active listening':

> Many children, in different ways, suggested that how teachers listened and the social context of being listened to was of crucial importance: 'Take more time to actually listen. Ask us in comfortable situations, not in front of other people.' (McCluskey, 2013, p. 292)

The principle is that the person does fundamentally recognise what is good for them and, given the right environment, will always move toward that good and/or generate the context to foster that good. Under the name of self-actualisation, this principle is described by Maslow (1943), but, it seems to me, is more fully experienced in the work of Carl Rogers, whose work I shall describe in greater detail shortly. In the context of this library memory, meanwhile, we encounter these questing young persons, whose explorations of their bodily limits (in a safe environment) are met with an imposition of scarcity. The question of proper authority, due process, communication, and respect all remain unanswered. Again, perhaps the little huddle was being disrespectful of the purpose of their neighbours. How was this discussed or resolved? Only by means of a short-circuiting of their involvement in a book. What, I wonder, was the book for? Maybe it had been purchased against the librarian's own judgement, taste, or ease? If so, then now that librarian was able to turn to their line-manager and say something along the lines of: *I told you so.*

If this force, self-actualisation, really does push our personal growth, guiding each set of interactions within an ever-shifting environment, then the question might well be one of *tools*.

The concept of 'tool' triggers a memory of a series of illustrations demonstrating how 'Early Man' struck stone with stone in order to make things. As this memory of an illustration is active, a number of observations are made: I can smell the book, the gentle rot of its glue; I know its size and feel its weight. My childhood environment is drawn up around me before receding, as it did when I was a child; I am sinking into the intent book scrutiny with my childhood I, and I myself now enter into the flint tool-making exercise with 'Early Man'. It is all a reaction to visual material, rather than any accompanying text. I can feel my nakedness in the world, the heat, my hands hefting the weight of this inquiry; stone. Behind me there is a cave, before me, rocky terrain; a group of hominids making noises is moving around me, and yet my awakening mind focusses intently on the flint in my hand. Surprisingly, rather than the rough boulder outline, its 'within' is visible. The 'within' is the tool, already arriving from out of its exterior form. What is more, the uses of the tool are also there: if this rock becomes the tool it is meant to become it will help me sharpen wooden sticks, the wooden sticks will help me kill animals, the animals will provide food, clothing, more tools, and this new becoming tool as yet in the rock will also help scrape clean flesh from bone. By envisioning rock becoming tool, this 'Early Man' has seen his whole existence become more efficient, more viable. If the insight into the inside of the rock can be shared horizontally amongst the community (and historically we presume this happened), then species development - evolution - is underway.

This olfactory book memory has triggered a cascading metaphoric description of self-actualisation and learning. The rock could not 'tell', nor 'Early Man' be instructed, and yet learning has taken place, enabled by the material relationship. One can see also the importance of that grunting background group; although they do not directly participate, they catalyse the moment, and the becoming tool works for them as much as for its author.

Memory is a fixing of points but also a mental space that may be manipulated, tested, turned around and inspected (Yates). It erects around itself the context, a physically experienced space, and yet simultaneously the content is displayed. Memory is experienced both in its physical and psychological impact. Further, the memory itself holds further memory (as I describe 'Early Man' the opening sequence of *2001: A Space Odyssey* - by Stanley Kubrick - irresistibly starts up, hovering over the imagery as an additional possibility). A contextual scaffolding is generated and one may enter into this construct to discover another array of the remembered.

Imagine the same stone-banging scenario in a slightly more sophisticated society. There is the tool, the rock in my hand: it needs only to be revealed, but the shaman comes out of the cave and says: *No, no, now no. That is not at all what the stone is for.*

Memory, therefore, is able to swiftly and neatly stitch together different reading experiences: one of absorption, the other of a curtailed group discussion.

In my experience this latter parental 'no' and the 'not listening' that accompanies it has not been limited to the childhood library life ...

I was working in a major university library on an issue desk. My normal role was in the specialist architectural department, but I was covering in a much larger section and was therefore a stranger, somewhat, to its protocols. This library stocked a range of one-hour loans. It was exam time and the collection was being tested by the sense of urgency this entails. There was only one copy of one particular book left. It had just come back but had not yet been shelved, and therefore was not allowed to be loaned. Could this rule be avoided if urgent circumstance asked? I was not in a position to say, and yet two people now wanted this one book (which neither was allowed to touch until shelved). They *needed it now*. To stir into the mix, one of the people wanting the book lived in the same house as I. This was difficult. The other person wanting the book knew this co-tenant also, having studied alongside him throughout their course. They could both actually see the book. Only the desk and myself stood in between. *Listen*, they said, *we **need it**. We can work it out together. Please ...*

With the great wisdom and authority of a person new to the job I explained that I would inform my line manager, who most certainly should be able to resolve this matter. The head librarian responded promptly, came out from her office, picked up the book and returned to her office with the book. Not once did she look at the imploring students, and nor was I required to explain the situation further. When I came into work the following day this one-hour loan item was still safely parked within the inner sanctum, causing no more disturbance.

Doubtless my view on this was skewed, or limited at least, for I was not seeing how the proper library concern was henceforth a question of securing further copies and perhaps conferring with the programme area as to whether or not this title was really required as a one-hour loan. I had heard *but we can work this out together* - and yet in spite of these two reasonable voices there were perhaps half a dozen more troublesome calls coming up behind them. The librarian had need to feed everyone, not a few.

The user demands, the seeker seeks, the gap is to be filled. A feeding model. Can feeding and knowing, consuming and learning, be seen as comparable? Learning is the wholly new and the always possible. The quandary for education, therefore, is: how in the light of this newness can learning be taught? The pedagogical materials are all drawn from other peoples, other times; no matter how contemporary, the taught subject is past - and yet the pedagogical experience one hopes to instil is entirely of this moment, and it is for this person's learning. (Although that grunting surround of hominids are surely participating in the learning, even if not directly.) There is, then, a contextual disjointedness to teaching and learning: the two phases are simultaneously intimate and entirely distinct. Vygotsky posits a Zone of Proximal Development in order to accommodate this. Social interaction is central to cognitive development, and teaching as sanctioned social interaction is a scaffolding for preparedness.

Human learning presupposes a specific social nature and a process by which children grow into the intellectual life of those around them.

> When the school child solves a problem at home on the basis of a model that he has been shown in class, he continues to act in collaboration … this aspect of collaboration – is invisibly present. It is contained in what looks from the outside like the child's independent solution of the problem. (Vygotsky, quoted in Daniels, 2001, p. 65.)

The learner's own character development and psychology - this preparedness for personhood - are not directly taught, but the collaborative shapes around that development are.

Scaffolding as a metaphor has the temporal advantage of being movable: it has no pretence of permanence. The metaphor then shades into accommodation, and we are able to talk of taught space as a welcome shelter. One enters this shelter with agreement to respond to the good hospitality with a giving of oneself in the same way that a traveller shares stories. Education thus becomes a mutually enriching exchange. At once scaffolding and hospitality: does this not seem an amenable description of the library as a collaborative space? Objectively it is an arrangement of objects; subjectively it is a theatre of memory in which players must play in order to stitch together their robes of meaningful meaning.

In other words, the library is a phenomenal field and, in an educational environment, it is called to be pasture, a consumable field. If the library user is to become a learner, a dynamic interaction is required – chewing cud at the very least! There are, of course, various degrees of hunger and different modes of curiosity. The library service may be skilled in a particular manner, geared toward satisfying a particular hunger. Nonetheless, the preparedness of the learner may not always, and will certainly not automatically always, fit the habitual functioning of the simplest institutional feeding mode.

Carl Rogers saw the development of fully-functioning persons not as the result of great expert skill and some chance but as sheer inevitability given the correct environmental conditions. In the therapeutic context the person themselves discovers their personhood; the patient knows best their route to healthy functioning and the environment which they require. In an educational context, significant or experiential learning

> *has a quality of personal involvement.* – the whole person in both his feeling and his cognitive aspects being in the learning event. *It is self-initiated.* Even when the impetus of stimulus comes from the outside, the sense of discovery, of reaching out, of grasping and comprehending, comes from within. *It is pervasive.* It makes a difference in the behaviour, the attitudes, perhaps even the personality of the learner. *It is evaluated by the learner.* He knows whether it is meeting his need, whether it leads toward what he wants to know, whether it illuminates the dark area of ignorance he is experiencing. The locus of evaluation, we might say, resides definitely in the learner. *Its essence is meaning.* When such learning takes place, the element of meaning to the learner is built into the whole experience. (Rogers, 1969, p.5. Emphasis in the original.)

Even as a stone tool must come forth from gross material as it imprints its possibility on an awakening mind, so is the fully-functioning person such a potential. How is it, then, that the apparent inevitability of the psychological whole person has been, to say the least, historically a patchy affair? In the vicissitudes of childhood one develops differing loci of evaluation. At a certain stage these may be appropriate collaborations - a co-constructed space of meaning and suitable adaption to the environment - but, going forward, they are always mismatched because, rather than adapt as the environment changes, they become a fixed function within the psyche. That initially fruitful collaboration between a teacher and learner, or a parent and a child, may persist to such an extent that the invisible partner is always present: perhaps volubly so, dogmatically so. Collaboration ceases and a dictatorship takes hold. A fixed function within the psyche, the invisible partner, is now making judgements on behalf of the present, and, furthermore, making demands on the present reality so that it is expected to fit an internal reality. A new reality will always be just that – new – whereas the internal scripts or commentaries are always familiar (overly so). In this situation of mismatch a learner experiences incongruence: they cannot be true and cannot trust their own learning experience; not speaking truthfully within their own self (or across their many inner personifications [Rowan, 2010]), a person cannot properly receive, never mind assess, the full spectrum of current information.

The person-centred approach is a means of re-evaluation but it does not move in as an intervention: the person is not turned into a medical object but matched as a trusted subject.

> The individual has within himself or herself vast resources for self-understanding, for altering his or her self-concept, attitudes, and self-directed behaviour – and these resources can be tapped if only a definable climate of facilitative psychological attitudes can be provided. (Rogers, 1986, reproduced in Kirschenbaum, 1989, p. 135.)

Rogers states that, given these core conditions, 'facilitative psychological attitudes' (Rogers, 1986), growth and healthy functioning are an unavoidable movement of the person. There may be specific tools or techniques that need to be introduced in facilitating the movement, but it is the person that recognises the need and moves toward its satisfaction. In an educational context this introduction of tools or techniques would be part of the learning mediation: while the teacher – or library – may well have access to these mediated objects, the motivational force between learner and learning nonetheless remains with person. The core conditions are:

Congruence – described as realness or genuineness.

> There is a close matching, or congruence, between what is being experienced at the gut level, what is present in awareness, and what is expressed ... (Rogers, 1986)

Unconditional Positive Regard – described as acceptance, respect, caring deeply and as a true concern for the individual.

Empathy – an *as if* quality wherein it is possible to trust the perception of the other's world as if one were experiencing that world; the meaning and feeling of that experiential quality becomes apparent (Rogers, 1986).

> Empathy implies a continuing desire to understand from the client's perspectives, regardless of one's own view, experiences, values. (Connolly, accessed April 2013)

Recent studies have discovered remarkable properties associated with empathy. Where empathy is present in the physician-patient relationship there is significant increase in positive clinical outcomes. It has also been shown that those who perceive themselves to be empathised with have a changed brain response to stress and an increase in pain tolerance (McGlashen; Sarinopoulos).

Again, recent reports from hospital clinical practice have highlighted the success of the Schwartz Center Rounds, a person-centred group focus meeting, in re-motivating medical and care professionals across all grades and roles. Goodrich reports how the focus is to 'care for the caregiver through a supportive work environment that treats them with the same dignity and respect that they are expected to show patients and families'. Once more it is noted that 'higher empathy is related to lower stress' (Goodrich, p.1, accessed May 2013).

The King's Fund published *Patient-Centred Leadership: Rediscovering our Purpose* as a direct response to findings of the Francis Inquiry (2013). The King's Fund particularly recommends valuing the person, staff and patient, and listening to the patient and their support networks (family, friends, care advocates). These are core Rogerian principals. The shame is that these calls are anything but new. In a 2001 White Paper, *Valuing People*, published by a previous government, person-centred planning is recommended:

> A person-centred approach to planning means that planning should start with the individual (not with the services), and take account of their wishes and aspirations. (*Valuing People*, p.56)

If we are to take anything from these clinical findings and recommendations then we shall need a sensible and meaningful mapping across process. Rogers himself applied this approach to education, management and organisational issues, and latterly to peace negotiations in South Africa and Northern Ireland. A library may not be dealing so dramatically with peoples' lives, but nonetheless we are dealing with an aspect of their living - and in the post-compulsory education sector we are in fact dealing with a vital, sometimes turbulent, stage in a person's development. The library may be that free, crucible-like space through which the transformative waters of young adulthood, learning, and new experience flow.

In Milltown College Library one sunny afternoon I pointed out to a more senior member of the team how cosy a particular couple seemed to be. He gasped in horror and sprinted between the stacks, bounded up a flight of stairs in two, and demanded that the couple – well – uncouple. There was no state of undress involved, just much entwining of limb and meeting of lip. The library signs ask for mobiles to be turned off, no food or drink, and remind everyone to act respectfully in a study area. As yet no new sign has been made: No Snogging.

On another occasion, C., a tutor who works with the FE provision, expressed some surprise at her rediscovery of how different the second-year students whom she normally taught were to the first. It was a busy period with each year group completing their final major project. The first years she described were far more 'needy'. They had to be reassured, guided, confirmed – and it was hard work. Just the short chronological gap between first and second year created in this young intake a great shift toward independence. In psychological terms they become more autonomous. This small insight has a potential impact on how the library imparts the skills and knowledge of library use: should inductions follow a two-phase strategy?

In Carl Rogers, it should be recalled, was a trained scientist. He observed this movement toward growth, development and healing in his clients and put his observations under empirical scrutiny and the approach remains a proven success in many cases (Cooper). This is not to say that the approach is uncontested, or that alternative approaches are invalid. Even therapists who were accounted Humanist Psychologists, as Rogers was, suggested that his optimistic view of the self-actualizing human might benefit from acknowledging a greater complexity:

> Does not Rogers' emphasis on rationality, and his belief that the individual will simply choose what is rational for him, leave out a large section of the spectrum of human experience, namely, all the irrational feelings? Granted that it is not 'exquisitely rational' to bite the hand that feeds you, yet that is just what clients and patients do – which is one reason they need therapy. And furthermore, this anger, aggressiveness and hostility, often express the patient's most precious effort toward autonomy, his way of trying to find some point at which he can stand against the authorities who have always suffocated his life – suffocated it by 'kindness' as well as by exploitation. (May, quoted in Rowan, 2001, p.31.)

This encounter with rage under a regime of kindness is worth pondering a little longer, for does not the attentive library service, for example, always strive to be kind? Or if not, then the functioning service needs always to show the rational workings of its system: The loan period is ... the fine is ... this item can be renewed, and so on. Every month, however, there are people who 'forget', 'lose', or mark, soak, rip or otherwise destroy books. (I have seen items returned that have clearly gone skateboarding, great tangents ground off the book's spine much in the manner of a schralped skater's elbow. Strangely, these books were re-shelved as if nothing untoward had happened.) In other words, any system must be designed in expectation of a certain amount of aggression, even if that aggression is passive aggression. No amount of rationality and clarity is ever likely to be sufficient to elicit an entirely clear and rational use of the service or system, and this holds in the library as much as in any other human institution.

While discussing the possibility of a person-centred library with N. and T. it was precisely this point of how to deal with aggression that suggested an ethos rather than a fully person-centred approach. The call of unconditional positive regard is precisely 'unconditional'. In order to run a service however it is presumed that one must set conditions: The loan period is ... the fine is ... etc. Nonetheless, should the ethos be *toward* the person, should it be an 'enabling style' (Mansell; Beadle-Brown), then those negotiations which inevitably arise around contested fines/losses/damage must put persons, not the fine/loss/damage, at the centre of the negotiation. And, to be real about this, in such negotiation there is the personage of the library, all those service concerns, represented by a staff member, who is also a person, and the person of the library user. This means there will be more than two people in this negotiation. There may also be all those hidden narratives to contend with – *they are a problem* – *why am I here* – etc. If the staff member of the library is not sure of their own condition of worth they may judge the situation around them by *how they imagine* some other person, a manager perhaps, would judge although such conjecture is fundamentally impossible. The library user's own locus of evaluation may not be within themselves, so they could be fantasising any number of alternatives that would alleviate their responsibility for being in the present.

We have touched on education as mediation (Vygotsky). In the above-described the two present people could each be object and subject, the one gaining knowledge from the other, while the mediating artefact (positioned at the apex of the triangle if we imagine this as a diagram) is the library in the institution with all its attendant (and clearly articulated) codes. Unfortunately it may be all too possible to scramble all these codes through another triangular description: the Karpman Drama Triangle.

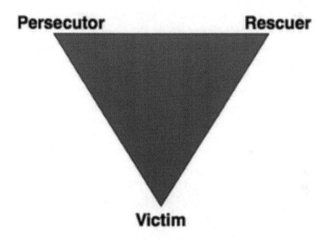

The Karpman Drama Triangle by Paul Ryder, from Wikimedia Commons

We may imagine the institution as persecutor, the 'good cop' staff member as rescuer and the library user as occupying the victim position. The bizarre truth about such scripted positions is that the victim script is driving this dynamic. The victim must be victim in order to be rescued. As the rescuer rescues, they force the victim from their position, all involved take up a new script position, and a drama occurs.

While such barely conscious games are playing themselves out there is a crucial lack of awareness. These are persona games, actors, and while quite often the drama can be very distracting, complexly absorbing, it is also horribly inefficient, time-consuming and sometimes simply painful. Without awareness of how the moment is structured, then the full range of other options will remain elusive.

A Milltown College library staff member runs the overdue notices on a regular basis. Over the arc of the academic season he has noticed what appears to be a regular pattern of relationship between seriously overdue library loans, an inability to establish meaningful contact with – and here pauses. He was going to say 'the offender', he explains, but given the context he now realises how loaded this language is, violent even. A transgressor, the offender; already the person is lost behind a prejudging set of association. The person, then, who has very overdue items, who has not responded to email alerting service or paper notice or the stern warning letter, is often also a person who is about to or already has withdrawn from their college programme. He wonders if an empirical study could be made before going on the suggest that often the withdrawal from education, as he sometimes discovers only afterwards, is related to ill-health, anxiety disorders, economics or chaotic family situations. Perhaps all the above at once - which then puts the matter of few books in some perspective. There are occasions, however, when one of their family or a member of the teaching faculty steps into this circuit and explains some circumstance. They act as a proxy between the library and the distressed student. By establishing a new quality of communication the matter can be resolved. Without such two-way communication the library system is doomed to repetition: TripTropTripTrop. Who's that trotting on my bridge!! TripTropTripTrop ...

N. makes the point that people will feel intimidated by the library but they will also be excited in response to it. People will have all sorts of reactions which are uniquely their own from a fluid, dynamic sense of themselves. The library service cannot actually avoid this as this response is the person's own responsibility, but, N. continues, the library can offer an environment where users are held and accepted in learning. Rather than 'rules' the service has boundaries. It is against these boundaries and the ethos of the library being there for the library users' needs that the staff can continually check themselves: How did I react to that? Did they prompt me to jump to conclusions? Were we listening?

So, the library staff member continued, it is in this context that we need to ask: can there be a simple structure put in place that is not just about transmitting information - X items late by Y days - and is not solely a matter of conveying threat - X items late by Y days will cost you Z. Such equations may look perfectly reasonable to their authors, but it is not possible to predict how they are received.

A metaphor from sense-making methodology is brought to mind: 'the studies assumed that the information brick was being thrown into the empty bucket' (Dervin). Clearly the library user is not an empty bucket: the whole point of using the library is to ensure one's bucket is at least partially full! Moreover, the anecdotal findings of Milltown College suggest that after a certain period of non-communication or stalled activity on the library account it is probably that bricks thrown in will be met by a storm of activity rather than an empty rattle:

> When you change the power differential in a class, you realize that students and professors become something different. They become more than people playing different roles. They become whole persons with thoughts, feelings, and behaviors which are fully taken into consideration. (Motsching-Pitrik and Santos, p. 17.)

A marketisation of the student body alters the balance of expectations. We have already met the feeding metaphor in the context of the library, and this same method of understanding the pedagogic contract can be applied to post-compulsory education as a whole. The stated aim of the BIS report *Students at the Heart of the System* is 'to put more power in the hands of the consumer' (2011). The student and consumer are accounted as one, and thus the whole sector is deemed a market, replete with branding strategies, products, and, of course, compelling testimony as to the quality of said product in the form of league tables and numerous surveys.

> Students widely buy into the idea of consumer sovereignty. Often inadvertently, this stance acts to reduce the potential value that studying at degree level can offer; for example, many students will opt to satisfy often whimsical personal tastes and preferences, rather than immerse themselves in the ambiguity and angst of deep learning … (Molesworth, et al. p. 233.)

It is in this seemingly fickle environment that the term 'student-centred' is promoted as a good. Outside the Rogerian context what may this mean? Can the student demand a pass as right because that is what they have paid for? Might the BA be purchased as an impulse buy, like a perfume or perhaps a tattoo? How will the scaffolding surrounding the preparedness for learning be reshaped to accommodate a more self-consciously privileged person? Clearly the learner is indeed a consumer: the manner in which the institutions are funded makes this unavoidable. Perhaps the question is, are they a consumer first and a learner only second, or vice versa? Or, by foregrounding this element of choice and expectation, do institutions actually prepare the ground for a participatory experience? It can no longer be acceptable for the paying customer to be held at a distance while dollops of fact and/or opinion are 'banked' in their person. Education as banking is the counter-concept, derived from Paulo Freire, to that of pedagogy as liberation. The active consumer of education may agree that they are not

> abstract, isolated, independent, and unattached to the world.
>
> [...]
>
> Authentic reflection considers neither abstract man nor the world without people, but people in their relations with the world. (Freire, p.81)

It is interesting to see how Freire's *authentic* non-alienated reflection has become refocussed as a strong brand word: the desirable *authentic experience* offered by ...

Education can function as being about getting the facts to get the degree to get the job. And post-compulsory education must be able to genuinely provide for both elements; employability and transformative learning. If the stress of this fault line falls mainly along the delivery of teaching programmes (or teaching and/or facilitation), the library is certainly not exempt from these tensions. The depth and breadth of a collection is, without doubt, worth promoting: it is a selling point. Is it possible for the library to be a free space for reflection, communion and becoming, while simultaneously recognising it is an easily accessible depository of correct and necessary data?

Is the institution 'student centred' because they, the students, are the financial fuel in this particular machine? Is the student therefore a monetary unit? Is the institution 'student centred' because this is code for image management, with the student required to be correctly displayed in any public correspondence? Perhaps these questions veer unduly toward the cynical but, again, there is an also/and running along the self-same ground. The best possible advertisement for any educational institution cannot be drawn from strategic portfolio or brand conference. 'It is by their fruit you shall know them'; an actual, vibrant, creative and visibly talented body of graduates is the convincing sign which will attract further consumers.

Student-Centered Learning is a personally significant kind of learning that integrates new elements, knowledge, or insights to the current repertoire of the learner's own resources such that he or she moves to an advanced constellation of meaning and resourcefulness. (Barrett-Lennard, quoted in Motschnig-Pitrick and Santos, p.4.)

There is always a cost to implementing change. If a person-centred library is to flourish then, it is suggested, a preparedness for learning would proportionally flourish. The library may even rebrand as *The Zone of Proximal Development*. Even so, for collaboration and co-constructed meaning to take root, person-centred action cannot be a mere proclamation. A linked series of goal-orientated actions is required that reaches from top to bottom of the organisation, with an attentiveness to checking and 're-checking on what is working and what is not working' (Smull, et al., p.4-5).

There is sometimes a cost to even suggesting change. For some situations it seems that to merely contemplate difference is far worse than the actual process of changing. In such a state even suggestions of a suggestion arouse suspicion and consequently aggression (usually passive), resistance and accusation. All the verbing of a negative processing: *digging in, making a stand*. This rhetoric may be slyly resentful or heroically barricaded, but in either case it is against a verbing of doing, flowing, fluxing, discovering or moving. An equal, if not greater, amount of energy may be invested in the former, more truculent, way. As in the drama triangle, the resisting mode demands that all other characters (and again the person is reduced to a role) engage in the designated destiny of 'with us or against'. Awareness becomes uncreative 'focus' and cognitive power is moved toward a nomenclature of stating positions. Self-actualising flux, the listening to persons, any change at all is now subtly removed from present activity.

Hearing, as Dervin argues, cannot be presumed from the sheer fact of transmission. Transmission and reception are mutually engaged or they are irrecoverably dysfunctional. To hear, listening is required. To speak, listening is required. To listen, meaning must be available and sought after. Which said, we again swing round to the question of the possibility of clear communication. In order to properly judge the successful functioning of an institution one has recourse to a whole new array of experts – the learning body – the person who knows in their own person how best to achieve their goals. 'Without partnerships, the inefficiencies increase' (Smull, et al., p.8).

The verbing of Sense-Making and the process of person-centred planning and action indicate that communication is a collaborative reality - the *doing* reality of a Zone of Proximal Development. The self is participatory and thus fundamentally weighted toward the necessity of the relational journey, the library journey, the learning person journey. One of the necessaries of the necessity of relationship is listening.

If a library is to hold a person-centred ethos, that ethos must develop creatively from within the library. Person-centred thinking and action develop from the ground up, but cannot suffice unless the ground-up also meets a top-down action in a manner both constructive and engaged. Following Michael Smull's terms, the whole body is to be looking for what needs to be celebrated, sharing good practice, and changing what is not working. As the library and its staff itself meet with the core conditions of realness, esteem, and empathy, so in this courageous move does it model for all its relationships the type of relating it expects to both provide and receive. Would this change be sufficient to impact on the number of books lost, stolen or damaged? Would this alter both the quality and the quantity of the interactions between library staff and library user, or indeed between library user and library user? Markers will need to be placed so as to measure how far the dunes shift. Strategies of relating may be devised; art exhibitions within the library, new patterns of pedagogy, and different circuits to alert users to services' agreed boundaries.

Then someone may say:

Stop, pot, stop! And at last the porridge stopped.

So they all joined in to clean the floor apart from the ogre, who made the coffee.

A note

Milltown College is fictional, an amalgam of several institutions the author has experienced. Nonetheless the conversations were genuine and experienced with immense gratitude - thanks:

N. and T. – College counselling staff

C. – Tutor

G. – Tutor

A. and K. – Learning difference support tutors

and every member of library staff ever encountered.

Afterword by Garry Barker

Dear Nick

As a young boy growing up in Dudley in what was then Worcestershire, I discovered the town library in about 1957 or 1958. In the approximately four years between first going inside what was a somewhat daunting classical building and my entry into Dudley Boys Grammar School, I discovered something wonderful. Worlds of ideas and stories that could transplant me into the past, the future, into strange and different countries and into the presence of people that sometimes frightened me and sometimes intrigued me. In the background was a quiet librarian, who would watch me wondering the shelves, and who would every now and again offer advice. I didn't realise what was happening, she was simply educating me at my own pace and allowing me to be an immersive learner. She never said something was off limits or a boring read, but she had a sense when I was getting sated with something. I had read virtually every Jules Verne in the place, when she simply suggested I now have a look at H G wells. Reading was random and often influenced by the images on the covers. H Rider Haggard stories always offered that thrill of exotic adventure whilst John Buchan could bring it all back home.

I don't think I've changed that much. But I don't go into libraries very much. What has made the difference is the internet and a salary. I was until I moved my base up to the college's newer site a regular user of the college library and I could make my way round the shelves by memory. The fact that the library was on the ground floor meant that you had to pass it on your way out and in and therefore were constantly reminded of something or other that you felt you had to read. The other issue was as I was a part-timer and for many years I couldn't afford to buy books, but even so I did, but not as much as when I started to deliver contextual studies materials.

So what changed? The first thing was the advent of internet buying. If I was thinking about a subject I wanted to keep the books related to it for long periods and refer to them when I wanted. Internet buying was a fast and cheap solution to this. I also liked to be able to show students or read from these books and I'm not a very good planner. Not to the extent of ordering books well beforehand and remembering to take them back etc. I also found that students were similar, so as I developed dissertation tutorial responsibilities I would 'loan' these books to students, often with a feeling I was never going to get a book back, but with a sense that at least the person I was giving it to might learn to love it, or cherish its contents. The days of the 1950s are now long gone. As a boy there were few other distractions and things were not out there to be collected. The nearest to owning personal property like books was probably the trade cards in Brooke Bond tea, but these were free and you swapped them with your mates. Now students expect to own things. iPods, computers, phones etc., are all expensive items that they own and they will have been given many books as children. A book therefore seems not so special nowadays, so you have to make a book special. This is why I have over the last 10 years simply given them away as gifts. I've given hundreds of books away over the years as the library itself may itself testify, as I gave my last collection to them as I finished my final year as a contextual studies lecturer. I think books are special, so special that they ought to stand outside the Capitalist system. Each one as it is written and then read, passes on in a unique vessel, human thoughts frozen in language. What then should be the best way to pass these idea vessels on? As you have written, centring a library around do's and don'ts and making late book returns subject to fines perhaps breaks the magical bond between the reader and the text. Either the books should all be free, or you chain them to the shelves. Introduce students to the gift economy, get them to see that quantitative easing isn't just to do with putting more money into the economy, it can be about getting everyone to actively share.

You point to the library's pastures, and these are by implication both pastoral and pastoral. Students need to graze the shelves as well as library staff offering professional advice at the right time. What is though often experienced by individual students at gut level is often a tightening of the stomach muscles as they confront a set of learning outcomes that have no link to his or her actual experience. Communication with hundreds of different individuals on widely differing courses by using 'the brief' is actually insane. If we weren't so used to being straightjacketed we would realise it, but we have worn the restrictors for so long that they have become the norm and straightjacketed patients now dictate their own medicine as a cure-all for everyone. Unconditional positive regard and empathy are just words if we put into place inhuman systems. Again you have referred to the fact that planning should start with the people not the system. So what do I suggest in response to your text? Well one thing I do believe is that if you establish good will all will eventually benefit. Give the students trust. Provide spaces for them to be what they want to be and for those who find books challenging, free the text from the books.

So many students are frightened by academic text and put off by its dry tone, but when they hear it read out or paraphrased as a parable or fable, suddenly pennies drop and they want to read. I tried to spend as much time as I could reading out loud to students in my last years of teaching contextual studies and would still with the fine art students I now work with if I wasn't so timetabled into a task orientated curriculum. I well remember the response to Patrick Oliver reading Beckett or Flann O'Brian to the students, those books were gobbled up by some, and others would just remember the sound of the spoken words, in either case those books had been opened for them.

I mentioned Rilke and his connection with phenomenology when I saw you last. Poets will perhaps always make their way into our thoughts before philosophers step in to try and organize them. As an art college I would suggest we are more about offering possibilities than collecting information, therefore our books can be seen as random thoughts waiting to be realised by chance encounters. Can you as librarians facilitate these encounters and foster them as you learn to recognize those browsing youngsters' different needs?

The pedagogy of the art library is rarely discussed, but I also believe the whole structure of art and design pedagogy is also rarely approached with the rigour and open mindedness of earlier writers such as Anton Ehrenzweig. Impose a structure on the learners and they will learn the structure and not the subject of study. More students ask me about what the brief means than what their own work might possibly become. Can the repository of texts be a place for the re-discovery of self? Perhaps it's as always down to individuals. That quiet woman in Dudley public library who watched a young boy grazing the shelves had no other agenda than being a good human being. The gift she offered me is one that still keeps giving.

Regards Garry

Bibliography

Bayne, T. (2010) The Unity of Consciousness. Oxford: Oxford University Press. http://www.oxfordscholarship.com/view/10.1093/acprof:oso/978019921 5386.001.0001/acprof-9780199215386-chapter-1 Accessed April 2013.

Berne, E. (1964) Games People Play; the psychology of human relationships. London: Penguin.

Bates, M. (2010) Information Behavior. Los Angeles. CRC Press: http://pages.gseis.ucla.edu/faculty/bates/articles/information-behavior.html Accessed May 2013.

Carter, A. (1990) The Virago Book of Fairy Tales. London: Virago.

Connolly, P. The 'As If' Quality of Empathy. http://www.openoog.com/emp.html Accessed April 2013.

Cooper, C. (2008) Essential Research Findings in Counselling and Psychotherapy. London: Sage Publications.

Cornell University Person-Centered Planning. 2013 http://ilr-edi-r1.ilr.cornell.edu/PCP/course04.cfm Accessed April 2013.

Daniels, H. (2001) Vygotsky and Pedagogy. London: Routledge.

Davis, R.D. (1992). 37 Common Characteristics of Dyslexia. Dyslexia Association International: http://www.dyslexia.com/library/symptoms.htm Accessed May 2013.

Department for Business Innovation & Skills. (2011) Higher Education: Students at the Heart of the System. London: The Stationery Office.

Department of Health. (2001) Valuing People: a new strategy for learning disability for the 21st Century. London: The Stationery Office.

Dervin, B. (2003) Sense-Making Methodology Reader: selected writings of Brenda Dervin. Cresskill, NJ: Hampton Press Inc.

Dervin, B. (1983) Information as a User Construct: the relevance of perceived information needs to synthesis and interpretation. Published in: Ward, S. (ed.) Knowledge Structure and Use: implications for synthesis and interpretation. Philadelphia: Temple University Press.

Ellis, A. (1977) Handbook of Rational-Emotive Therapy. New York: Springer Publishing.

Francis, R. (2013) The Mid Staffordshire NHS Foundation Trust Public Inquiry. http://www.midstaffspublicinquiry.com/report Accessed May 2013.

Freire, P. (1970) Pedagogy of the Oppressed. London: Contiuum Publishing.

Garcia, I. et al. (2007) Listen Up! Person-centred approaches to help young people experiencing mental health and emotional problems. London: Mental Health Foundation. http://www.mentalhealth.org.uk/publications/listen-up/ Accessed April 2013.

J. Goodrich. (2011) Schwartz Center Rounds: evaluation of the UK pilots. London: The King's Fund. http://www.kingsfund.org.uk/sites/files/kf/field/field_publication_file/schwartz-center-rounds-pilot-evaluation-jun11.pdf Accessed May 2013.

The King's Fund. (2013) Patient-Centred Leadership: Rediscovering Our Purpose. London. The King's Fund. http://www.kingsfund.org.uk/publications/patient-centred-leadership Accessed May 2013.

Kirschenbaum, H.; V.L. Henderson (eds). (1989) The Carl Rogers Reader. New York: Houghton Mifflin.

Mansell, J; Beadle-Brown, J. (2003) Person-Centred Planning or Person-Centred Action? A response to the commentaries. London: Journal of Applied Research in Intellectual Disabilites. 2004 .

Maslow, H. (1943) A Theory of Human Motivation. http://psychclassics.yorku.ca/Maslow/motivation.htm Accessed April 2013.

McCluskey, C. et al. (2012) 'Take More Time to Actually Listen': students' reflections on participation and negotiation in school. Oxford: British Educational Research Journal. Vol. 39, #2, April 2013.

McGlashen, A. (2012) We Tolerate Pain Better When Doctors Listen. http://www.futurity.org/top-stories/we-tolerate-pain-better-when-doctors-listen/ Accessed May 2013.

Merleau-Ponty, M. (1968) The Visible and the Invisible. Evanston: Northwestern University Press.

Molesworth, M. et al. (2011) The Marketization of Higher Education and the Student as Consumer. London: Routledge.

Motschnig-Pitrik, R.; Santos, A.M. (2006) The Person-Centered Approach to Teaching and Learning as Exemplified in a Course in Organizational Development. www.zfhe.at Accessed May 2013.

O'Brien, J. (2003) If Person-Centred Planning Did Not Exist, *Valuing People* Would Require its Invention. London: Journal of Applied Research in Intellectual Disabilites. 2004.

Rogers, C.R. (1951) Client-centered therapy: its current practice, implications and theory. London: Constable and Company.

Rogers, C.R. (1969) Freedom to learn; a view of what education might become. Columbus, Ohio: Charles E. Merrill.

Rogers, C.R. (1986) A client-centered / person-centered approach to therapy. SEE p.135, Kirschenbaum.

Rowan, J. (2001) Ordinary Ecstasy: the dialectics of humanistic psychology (3rd edition.) London: Routledge.

Rowan, R. (2010) Personification: using the dialogical self in psychotherapy and counselling. London: Routledge.

Sarinopoulos, I. (2012) Patient-Centered Interviewing is Associated with Decreased Responses to Painful Stimuli: An initial MRI study – in Patient education and counselling. Philidelphia: Elsevier.

Smull, M.W. et al. (2009) Becoming a Person-Centered System. National Association of State Directors of Developmental Disabilities Services, Inc NASDDDS. http://www.nasddds.org/pdf/BecomingaPersonCenteredSystem-ABriefOverview.pdf Accessed April 2013.

Syngg, D; Combs, A.W. (1959) Individual Behaviour: a perceptual approach to behaviour. New York. Harper. UK Government. (2010) Equality Act 2010. https://www.gov.uk/equality-act-2010-guidance Accessed May 2013.

Yates, F.A. (1966) The Art of Memory. London: Pimlico.

Zipes, J. (1979) Breaking the Magic Spell: radical theories of folk and fairy Tales. Kentucky: The University Press of Kentucky.

The Winning Hand of Independence: Reviewing Literature / Alke Gröppel-Wegener

Reviewing literature is surely a key skill for any budding academic, but particularly for students engaged in postgraduate study. For about four years I have been teaching a research methods course for a number of Masters level humanities students, which gets assessed through a report on a research project of the students' choice which includes a brief literature review. Over the last two years in particular I have been getting an increasingly large number of annotated bibliographies instead of literature reviews (often referred to as 'literary reviews'). The teaching strategies and materials didn't change over that time period, but clearly students didn't quite understand the point of using this part of their report to discuss the themes and issues raised in the secondary sources they use. Instead this section often reads like the university equivalent of a finger painting put up on a fridge, saying "Didn't I do well? I read all three of those books and this was in them!"

But how best to explain the difference of reading a book and engaging with its content, putting it into context with the issues that your research is about, having the confidence to discard some bits of information because for your own context they are irrelevant?

I had been working with my undergraduates on a similar problem encouraging them to condense sources into greeting card formats to hone their skills of judging relevance to their own research – and this idea of the card – not quite a greeting card, but a playing card, clearly conceived in a very specific context (a suit, the order of the ranks) – seemed like a good visual to explain this idea.

The following text is the starting point of a new resource I will test with the students in the coming year, by giving them access to this text as well as piloting a literature review workshop where we will work on condensing secondary sources into a playing card form in order to be able to shuffle information and directly visualise the difference between the annotated bibliography and the literature review.

Working with secondary sources can be tricky.

Once you have found good ones – written by experts and located at an appropriate academic depth – it can be difficult to 'let go' of the source.
After all, very often all the information presented seems interesting and, if the writing is done well, the order makes perfect sense, too. But neither all the information, nor the order might be relevant in the context of <u>your</u> research ...

In academic writing there are different ways of presenting the information you gathered to your readers, the main ones being
the **Annotated Bibliography** on the one hand

   and the **Literature Review** on the other.

 But there is a huge difference between them ...

In a way you can imagine the information you get from a particular source as playing cards of the same suit.

When you open the pack,
they are ordered according
to their suit, the way they
were ordered by the author.

In a basic Annotated Bibliography, you present
your reader with what in Poker would be a
series of Straight Flushes –
cards of the same suit,
in sequence.
Just like they came

out of the pack.

In a Poker game,
that is quite a good hand.
When dealing with sources, this is a basic
summary of each source on its own – it tells your
reader what is in each source, possibly analysing
which are the important bits.

What is already
more interesting
for the reader is
you ordering the
information
according to what
is important in
your context, and
discarding the bits
that aren't.

In Poker this would be a series of Flushes.

And while in Poker this would be defeated by a Straight Flush, when comparing Annotated Bibliographies, the series of Flushes might rank higher, because you show your own analysis of the subject matter rather than staying with the order prescribed by the original author.

However, most of the time, readers are less interested in a summary of your sources than in what you have actually found out!

Oh, they want you to present relevant information – and tell them where you got that – but this needs to be tailored to your own context.

So for the reader it shows more of your understanding of the issues and debates if you put the issues and debates in context with one another.

In other words, you need to 'free' the information, issues and debates from the order the author put them in, because what the original author found important isn't actually what is most interesting to you –
    – thinking of the cards, maybe you don't need the suits, but rather the ranks.

Maybe you need
only even numbers ...

... or picture cards ...

... or just 3s.

So rather than describing every bit of
information (the individual card) in the sequence
of the suits (as prescribed by the author),

maybe you need to shuffle your deck
of information and swap your cards around,
discarding the information you don't need,

and collecting only
the bits that you <u>do</u> want.

If you are dealing with your sources in this way,
you are producing a Literature Review:
you need to go away from the prescribed order of
the author that you stick to for an Annotated
Bibliography;

you need to ignore the suits and try to find
information that deals with the same issues, so
similar card values.

In Poker that would be hunting
for Pairs, or, even better,
several Of A Kind.

And, as chances are that there is only a limited
amount of cards you can hold at any one time, it
does not make sense to keep all the cards.

Rather, you should decide what cards you need to
collect
  - the others can be discarded.
          Just like in a card game with very specific
                                            rules.

In academic writing you usually have a similar
limit (like a word count, for example). So you
need to decide the issues and debates you want to
focus on, and discard the rest, just like
unwanted cards.

You need to identify the information that is
relevant in each source and then present – and
discuss – them in the context of what other
authors wrote about the same issues.

  The trick is making the information independent
    of where it came from (while still referencing
  it, of course) and putting it into your very own
                                specific context.

          This way you can put the found bits of
information into context with each other, analyse
and compare them. You might even find pieces of
information that are wild cards – like Jokers in
                            some card games,
        they might fit into more than one context.

When you are ready to present the context of your argument in your Literature Review, you can order the cards as you want to – and while it is important to keep in mind (and reference) where they came from, i.e. which suit (or secondary source) – it is really your discussion of the information that is most interesting to your readers.

And when it comes to a Literature Review, that is a winning hand.

The Travellers

A virtual conversation between two artists / Inês R. Amado and Ximena Alarcón

We are two artists working around issues of interconnectedness of inner and outer journeys, through the use of dreams and of technology. For this publication, we are generating an article about our states of creating, of learning and of exploring technology, together with the effects and emotions that these produce. We are engaging in a technology-mediated dialogue (Skype, Google Drive, zoom microphone and video recorder) and sharing our dreams, to reach an all-inclusive understanding of these experiences involving the mind and the body, immersing them in a relational process.

We draw a connection between the body, the mind, consciousness, emotion and self-awareness, and have created a journey of "autopoesis" as addressed by the work of Umberto Maturana and Francisco Varela: a continuous exploration or production of ourselves. We are locating our journeys within a time frame unconstrained by the cognisant intellect, but nourished by the wisdom of the mind and interweaved by historical chances, when our mutual experiences overlap. We pause to explore aspects (creative, aesthetic, social, philosophical and poetical) that link these experiences. This process allows a flow of energy and information shared with each other.

> Vamos falar,
>
> dialogar,
>
> trocar,
>
> intercambiar,
>
> divagar ...

vamos sonhar!

Neste sonhar há realidade,

há criatividade,

prazer e lazer

Mas há também indagar, ponderar, há análise, sistema e co-produção.

Neste duplo sonhar há dar e receber, há trocar e alargar conhecimento e razão

Let's talk, dialogue, share, exchange, digress ... let's dream!
In this dreaming there is reality, creativity, pleasure and leisure
But there is also inquire, pondering, there is analysis, system and co-production.
In this double dreaming there is give and take, exchanging and expansion of knowledge and of reason.

Vamos a escuchar y explorar

Nuestras techno ilusiones
Nuestras cosmovisiones

Entretejiendo con lazos etéreos

Las razones   por las que hoy estamos aquí

Cuestionando nuestro *sentido* de pertenencia

Con nuestros *sentidos*

Razones para estar

Casa,   territorio,   eter

Sonido,
memoria,
lenguajes

Creaciones

Let's listen to and explore, our techno illusions, our Cosmo visions.

Let's interweave with ethereal wires the reasons why we are here

Questioning our sense of belonging, with our senses

Reasons to be ... Home, territory, ether ... Sound, memory, languages

Creations

Questions and answers
[28-02-2013, Leicester – St. Albans]

What were the first technologies that you used in your life?

Inês: This is a difficult one, as I had a phobia of technology. But I do remember as a teenager having a very basic photographic camera and a tape recorder. Computers however were something to be either frightened by or ignored, left to accumulate dust and cobwebs, (at the University of Hertfordshire, where I worked back in the early 90s).

For me to use a computer was something very difficult, but my camera and tape recorder, at that point, were great fun. Yes, I had a terrible feeling of worry and of dislike for the computer. I used the camera and a tape recorder all the time, as for the computer before 1997, hardly ever. 1996/7 is a very important marker of time, of space and of creativity, through a series of new and forbidding technologies I managed to do something that had never been done before.

Ximena: I did use radio transistors and tape recorder with radio. Also a yellow transistor radio that went incorporated into headphones. They all were very colourful: Sesame Street, and my red tape recorder. I loved all of these. I use to leave them on under my pillow to go to sleep. The tape recorder was my very useful technological tool that accompanied me to my community work. It was red, and had the perfect size and great power. Its design was beautiful. My father gave it to me on my 15 year old birthday. The transistor radios were part of my childhood, 70's and 80's. I used my tape recorder from 1987 until 2001, when I left my country. Now I am amazed thinking how these early relationships with technology influenced my work as an artist.

Which technologies allowed you to create?

I: Back in 1996/7 I had to use all sorts of technologies, including ISDN lines from BT, computers and other technologies which were extremely new then. It was through the process of using computing systems, video cameras and sound recorders, that I created *Sands in Time,* a piece of work composed of four very large sandblasted glass panels with a text in clear glass relief - the imaginary pages of an imaginary book - evoking the notion of renewal, regeneration and transformation in a natural and man made environments. This installation was the first live video immersive installation to be live on the Internet (1997).

There is a socio-historical connection between the Azores and London and I wanted to bring to the fore that connection as well as to question perceptions of time and space. The Internet was then, and still is, an incredible tool to address these perceptions as well as issues of dislocation and of displacement.

The live site-specific installation at Trinity Buoy Wharf Light House, in London, brought live video from the Azores via satellite (I was able to use three hours of the Middlesex Hospital's satellite connections, every day during three weeks).

Two Lighthouses

These images were layered and fused with other live images from Trinity Buoy Wharf and Canary Wharf. Each individual viewing the installation became an integral part of the work as if absorbed and immersed in between the two pages of a book. Thus all the elements that composed the work became one multi-layered, multimedia, and transatlantic experience.

Audience engagement, interaction, and participation are part of the material essence of the work hence activating the public beyond that of the passive observer and questioning both the role of the artist as well as the role of the viewer / participant / maker and challenging the work, through the involvement of the public, both in situ and through cyberspace, enabling a richer and more enlarged understanding of the situation in which the artistic phenomenon took/takes place.

Sands in Time

[Video *Sands in Time* http://vimeo.com/67122532]

X: In 1990 I used a Pentax photo camera, which I loved. My brother Cesar gave it to me as a present. It was my aesthetic foundation and I created audiovisuals derived from still images. Later I produced TV and radio. Although I never touched the editing audiovisual technology, I made decisions of sequencing, developing a rapid eye and ear.

In 1997 in Barcelona I learnt to program in Lingo to create computer screen based interactive multimedia. This experience helped me to identify myself as an artist. I was able to experiment with all media in a single machine, establishing relationships between actions and the material triggered by the user on an interface; it was like having a black canvas in a multimedia theatre. I was in charge of all the creation process, from the idea to the final production. I realised I had more control than before over the audiovisual material and was able to develop new aesthetic ideas; that fascinated me. I was able to break the linearity of audiovisual narratives and to express concepts going beyond the written discourse. When people experienced my work *Interactive Metro* (1998), I felt that this was an immersive experience for them and they were touched in a subconscious level. I interrelated two technologies: screen-based interactive multimedia (fragmented but cinematic), and the underground transportation system. This was the foundation for *Sounding Underground*[2] (2009).

---

[2] http://soundingunderground.org

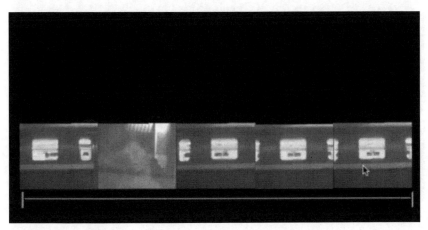

Sounding Underground

[Video *Interactive Metro* https://vimeo.com/51626952]

In 1998 I learnt history and technologies of sound art and used my Sony tape recorder to capture soundscapes. My fascination with listening, recording and mixing sounds was open to creative possibilities. I created my first sound installation *A to Z*[3] , inspired in memories of literacy. Internet was a good metaphor for connectedness but its slow speed and its aesthetics did not attract me. Years later, and parallel to my process of migration, Internet aesthetics and bi-directionality, became very attractive to me. I thought that through *Sounding Underground* – a virtual sonic environment that connects listening experiences in London, Mexico and Paris metros – many people could use the interface to upload their sounds.

---

[3] http://ximenaalarcon.net/sounds/A_to_Z_XAlarcon.mp3

Sounding Underground

The complexity of its technical realisation and the in-depth ethnographic process that informed the work suggested that individual experiences of listening deeply to a common underground infrastructure could extract essences of the space, and that the assemblage of it in a shared interface, could become an emotional catalyst for anyone who interacted with it on the web. The environment didn't need hundreds of data and people to accomplish its function. This perspective contradicts the accumulation of information experienced by social media, and makes a different intimate space to wonder. We are not linked and mediated only by technology but by something else: Jung's collective unconscious, which is present in interstitial spaces such as underground passages and the space of dreams.

Which technologies allowed you to play?

I: Today I find Skype an incredible tool with which I can be playful and creative. My computer today, unlike yesterday, is an extension of my creativity, by using different tools and programmes I am able to create video, sound and creative writing. I am very attracted to a combination of sound, object, and/or video. Issues of migration and of dislocation are always present.

Connecting ...

Facing the Other – Here and Now was a site/space-specific installation in Lisbon, Portugal, July 2011. The installation was inside a shipping container outside the entrance to Centro Cultural de Belém, the Cultural Centre of Belem. CCB is situated in the historic district of Belém in Lisbon from where the 'Age of Discovery' and colonial adventures were launched in the 15th century. (CCB was built to mark a new Portuguese adventure, succession to the European Union.) *Facing the Other – Here and Now* investigated and addressed notions of national identity, urban space and migration within the context of a former imperial society coming to terms with the political and cultural after-life of colonialism in its different facets. These issues related to the symbolic location of the containers in the historical district of Belém in Lisbon, a place marked physically and visually by buildings, gardens, museums, banners designs and symbols relating to the discoveries; the complex histories of trade and colonialism between coloniser and colonised.

Facing the Other – Here and Now

In 2012 I created **Relocated,** a sound and object installation work that reflected upon current issues within the EU. A united Europe where the unity seems to be only present in the obliteration of the individual and the individuality of each country. The orange together with the orange tree is a reminiscent and a reminder of those other objects extrapolated from Cyprus in days gone by. History does tend to repeat itself! In this piece I used the orange as a metaphor for a world where migration and globalization, dislocation displacement and relocation, conflicts and disputes, are second nature along with the demarcation of territories and pan-global hybridization. The orange is also used in this piece as an expression of temporality over time and space.

Installation, Cyprus

X: I like to play with sonic improvisation in networked performance. First in 2008, as part of the process with participants when creating *Sounding Underground*, I created *Listening and Remembering: networked improvisation for four commuters*[4]. This was a co-located improvisation where participants expressed memories with their voices, as they were triggered by the sounds of the metro; they interweave those through a common interface that allowed the recording and playback of theirs' as well as others' memories.

---

[4] http://artes.ucp.pt/citarj/article/view/27

Listening and Remembering: networked improvisation for four commuters

Continuing with my interest in real-time encounters between people and the spaces created by their interactions, now I'm exploring the 'in-between' space in the migratory context through telematic sonic performance and using the Deep Listening practice. *Letters and Bridges*[5], between Mexico City and Leicester, explored this space through letters that different migrants have received from people they love; they exchanged also a letter with their counterpart about feelings towards the place where they live. Inês, I reconnected with you when you exhibited *Relocated* and you participated in *Letters and Bridges* as a performer and Deep Listener! This was a great experiential connection between our works. *Migratory Dreams*[6] interrogates the space of migration as manifested in the dreams of Colombians living in London and in Bogotá. The free space of dreams allowed sharing between people from the same country to express their experiences of migration in a transcendental manner.

---

[5] http://networkedmigrations.wordpress.com/letters-and-bridges/

[6] http://networkedmigrations.wordpress.com/migratory-dreams/

Migratory Dreams. Photo by Laura Criollo

Being overwhelmed with information
[28-04-2013 Leicester – St. Albans]

X: This week was very hard for me, in terms of an overload of information, on Wednesday I don't know how many emails I received and how many I responded to but it was really really hard, and I finished very late and went to bed at 1am. That night I didn't have dreams, it was like my internal hard drive, my brain was completely out, worried, overwhelmed with everything I had to do …

Yesterday a student told me something funny and interesting; she asked me how am I, and I said that my startup disk was full, and she said 'you should remove some memories of childhood and that will open space', this resonated with me. Well, I guess the transistor radios are memories of childhood incorporated in my experience. Our memories are experiences.

I: Yes, experiences that mark and define, although they may hold us back and not allow us to dream.

Having dreams

Having dreams is a faculty that we humans share with other 'warm blooded animals (birds and mammals)' (Ione, 2005, p.71). As noted by Lewis, and according to Dr. Michel Jouvet it seems that 'we need regular, periodic dreaming to preserve our very individuality, and that dreaming is a time for essential genetic reprogramming within the brain' (idem). During sleep our subconscious is free, unguarded and adept to bring together past, present, and future, as dreams seem to be timeless, unimpeded by the cognisant intellect. Bodies are not the structure that we might have imagined, but are a process - change is our continuous reality - and as Persian Sufi mystic Rumi states: "we have come spinning out of nothing". One could say that we are molecules of dreams.

"The mind is an embodied and relational process that regulates the flow of energy and information, consciousness included. Mind is shared between people. It isn't something you own; we are profoundly interconnected." (Daniel Siegel, quoted in Patty de Llosa, 2006) We cannot survive without dreams, just as we cannot fulfil our journey without the memory of our beginnings.

Sharing Dreams

First dream: The flock of birds and the ethereal embodiment
[04-04-2013, Leicester - St. Albans]

X: I am going downstairs at four in the morning; this is the time and light when in this hemisphere the world is waking up. I am in a house where there is a window or a door to the back garden; it is more like a yard, where there are clothes hanging to be dried by the sun. What I see is a flock of ducks, and it is massive and the wings and the flapping and the sound that they make is so beautiful. I say, in the dream, that I haven't heard this sound before; and I also say that it is one of the most beautiful sounds I have ever heard, and I want to record it at the same time that is happening; but I don't find a microphone to record it, and I call Ron and try to explain what happened and when I show the scene to him the birds have gone. All that was left was the movement of the clothes that are hanging.

[Please watch Video 1. Presence
http://innovativelibraries.org.uk/Presence.mov]

I: What is your feeling in relation to the clothes?

X: It was scary, because I thought there was a person or a presence there, like the perception of someone inhabiting the clothes, and there is a kind of sadness, and abandonment, it is like if I were missing things because of my rejection of technology, which I have been doing the last few years because it is harming my body (sitting long hours by the computer because of the amount of information).

My body hurts

         Little toes and little fingers hurt because of the computer

I want to read in an old fashion way

At the same time I am missing things that are beautiful to capture …

I: I think … when you were talking, what I was visualizing, was something much more ethereal, transient, and quite beautiful and in a way those clothes for me encapsulated that transient moment; because they stayed behind and, on one level, they were grounding the experience; but on the other, they were moving in the wind, and actually in a way continuing the movement of the birds that had flown away, in a way they were saying to you that, that unique moment was still present. So the clothes were the physicality or the embodiment of that moment, in terms of movement and of sound; and that moment is still present in your memory and that is something to be cherished.

[13-04-2013 St. Albans-Leicester]

I: I've been thinking of the amazing image of the birds singing and the residue of that singing to me is like an ethereal presence that actually is ethereal because it is so beautifully liquid, but not diluted, a presence that stays; the clothes bouncing, they recover and embrace that moment that is so important, they encapsulate it, they are an open arena for some continuous action. There is a parallel between that retrieved moment and us at this precise moment in time. Not physical but ethereal, metaphysical. I've been thinking of how to incorporate, absorb and also make it emerge through sound movement…

[Please listen to the audio: A Dream-Dream

http://innovativelibraries.org.uk/dream-dream.mp3]

Second dream: The house - temporal refuge - and the open space of the mind

[13-04-2013, St. Albans-Leicester]

I: I had a dream last night: It's been very difficult, a difficult dream …

The house …

What my dream was ... I was somehow picking up some plastic bags and some clear containers, they were like plastic drawers, they were partly damaged, I was picking these up, and someone came along, next to these things, there was a kind of ruin: the outer walls of a house without a roof, just standing there, this ruin doesn't have a ceiling but it has a door. And I went in because I didn't want to be seen, the person outside came along and locked the door, although I wasn't really frightened, I was assessing the situation and felt ... I think I felt humiliated. Then I saw that within the ruin there was a hole here, a square hole, and another there, thus I decided that I could climb up, by putting one foot on each of the holes, then, I somehow manage to get out and that's the dream.

There was something else, as I was picking the containers up they felt very specifically useful, I was collecting them to put materials to do some work with, some sculpture possibly, or maybe drawings whatever, I was visualising those boxes as the bases to tiding my materials up to make some artwork.

... someone at the door and the person locked me in. I was hiding away.

X: I like that you are active in the dream and thinking of survival resources and how some elements can help you to keep the things that you really need.

I: Yes, just different materials, that I have in the studio, and objects that I collect, and I think there were books as well.

---

[7] I invite Inês to amplify her dream. I am using practices inspired by Robert Bosnak's experience of Embodiment (2009), and Ione's teachings (2005) in creative power that ritual can bring from our dreams.

I escape and I don't know what happened next.

I don't have any memory about it.

A ritual[7]

X: Let's start from the point when someone locks the door: the trigger for you is to escape.

I: I am drawing … I am drawing trees in the room. I am pushing the walls out. It's soft now, almost like plywood, actually cardboard, oh, it's just like out of a box. I am stepping on it, I am waving good-bye to the house, to the ruin. I am in a forest or something. The sounds are lovely, there are birds… there are some ground animals, maybe moles, ferrets, something underground that I cannot hear, only perceive. There are peacocks on the trees. It's warmish, with lots of lighting. I am coming out into a field of green grass, and there are cows on it. I am just sitting down. I am touching the grass and the grass has dewdrops, and I am feeling the wet grass with my fingers. I am just letting go. I am just lying down now, and my arms are open and the sun is really shining, and I think now I am with you.

[Please watch video: Home

http://innovativelibraries.org.uk/Homevideo.mov]

X: I am opening the arms, and when I did that the sun came through my window …

I: We are extending, prolonging each other's thoughts, feelings and dreams.

Birds … house … when you asked me to extend the dream, you were accompanying and enabling me to lengthen the dream and to explore further thoughts and possibilities.

X: For me the house – home has become my body

Really, the house is my body, it is not these walls

All this is kind of impermanent.

I: I think belonging is the home and the home is the body and the body contains the mind. I think that to quite an extent you are describing the very essence of being in exile, and you know, we are as people that have come out our own country exiles, all of us, the migrant is an exile, no matter how we have come here; intellectuals or manual workers. And we are here there, and *nowhere*. We are *there* that is the ideal place, because we cannot be *There*. When we go back to our own countries… the feeling is: where is home, where is home?

[Please listen to audio file: Connecting

http://innovativelibraries.org.uk/ConnectingPoem.mp3]

X: I am looking forward for a time when we have a friendlier relationship with technology that is linked with the relationship we have with the earth. A balanced relationship; initiatives such as the new environmental phone, Fairphone, which profits will go directly to the miners, as part of a different kind of economic model.

I: We need systems that are recyclable, and ecologically sound. The accumulation of material goods has to stop. We have to readdress all these issues as we – the earth – cannot sustain this approach anymore.

X: We have to design systems, technologies, practices, routines that are very different from the ones that we have experienced. If we look at the history of our artistic experience in 1997, the technologies we used challenged us to achieve what we imagined and created. Then, we see 15 years later, that many of these ideas are technologically possible to do ...

Would you repeat the *Sands in Time* installation?

I: No, I don't think so ...

The space was so full of equipment. One massive area within the lighthouse was completely taken by the equipment; it was monstrous, there were pieces of hard technological gear that were so cumbersome... all of which have been replaced by software. But of course at that point I didn't know anything about how to handle it all. It was Dave who dealt with all the technical bits. I had the support of the Portuguese television, who were sending me live footage from the Azores, three hours every day, also Middlesex Hospital satellite time, and three dedicated ISDN lines from BT, which was quite unusual ...

The place where I was, at that point in time, was very different from yours. I was a sculptor. For me to handle that extremely technical project was rather overwhelming, a breakthrough, it was massive! I was at the time dealing with sculptural issues and addressing precisely the effect of producing more objects in a world already so saturated with objects. So this was shifting ground for me on so many levels. Working with live video and all the technologies necessary to support its various conceptual and physical needs was for me an exquisite experience, but tremendously difficult. I didn't have any barriers in conceptualising the piece, everything was possible because I was so naïve about what was or was not possible in technological terms. And that's how I managed to overcome 'impossibilities'; I had a concept, which I felt was sound ... issues of installation of site specificity had been addressed before within my work, so the remaining was basically resting on challenging technology, and relying on the expertise of Dave Lawrence who was my wonderful assistant/collaborator.

X: For me, *Interactive Metro* was a kind of prototype for something that I imagined was possible to do: people connected via webcams, in real time from different parts of the cities and they could project images from what was happening there; this is how we could perceive the sense of any city with the metaphor of the underground. Many things are buried; I was coming from communication sciences, and I was thinking that I was creating a new medium. I wanted at the same time a media art piece, and a medium of communication. When I looked at the existent technology, and at what I had in my mind, these visions didn't match, because of the aesthetics ... Internet was basically text. At that time, in Europe, artists were experimenting with streaming video. It took me ten years to clarify the idea, and find the core, which eventually was music. I had many ideas; eventually, I didn't do what I initially wanted, but I created a virtual environment that I feel good about and that defies this amount of information that we have to deal with. I didn't create a medium, but a space that is a catalyst of feelings. Without including thousands of samples and of people, this nevertheless represents a collective memory. When interacting, people connect with personal and collective feelings.

I: Reassessing your question, I wouldn't want to do it now because I also have moved on. However in *Sands in Time* I dealt with fundamental issues that I have been addressing throughout my career as an artist. Issues of temporality were really dealt with in a temporal format. Also the individual "I" was pushed out of the studio, out of my comfort zone, and thus enlarged and challenged into focusing on an inclusive, participative, physical and ethereal experience.

X: Yes, like you I feel that I have moved on. Although we work with different beginnings and materials, our work has many connections. And we have dealt with a large amount of information, data, and have been challenged by technologies. For example, even if I had made use of webcams, for my initial idea, I would have found that I had been acting as a big brother, observing every single aspect of the world, which is what Internet represents in relation to many corporate driven social media.

You focus on specific individual experiences and of course you use the media to extend the idea of connection.

I: Yes, from the individual to the collective.

X: My evolution has been towards telematic performance, as it allows a straight connection between individuals who have a reason to connect.

I: From the collective experience into the individuality of each experience …

References

Bosnak, R. (2007). *Embodiment, Creative Imagination in Medicine, Art and Travel*. East Sussex: Routledge.

Jouvet, M. (2001). The paradox of sleep: the story of dreaming. Translated by Laurence Garey. MIT Press, A Bradford Book

Ione [Lewis, C. I.] (2005). *Listening in Dreams*. IUniverse Books.

De Llosa, P. (2011). The Neurobiology of "We". *Parabola Magazine*.

Credits

The sound poem *Connecting* includes the file called Garden Evening, taken from freesound.org, and recorded by the user NML http://www.freesound.org/people/NLM/sounds/72932/

Information seeking and challenging the concept of the unreliable narrator: finding autism, finding the true self / Penny Andrews and Marika Soulsby-Kermode

Where we're coming from

It is hard to explain how constantly being challenged by the world about the way your brain works, the way you express yourself, and even something as basic as how your body moves, feels.

Can't you just stop that?

No.

Can't you just be normal?

No.

[Please watch the video Connecting Pictures on YouTube: http://innovativelibraries.org.uk/CP]

No one believed us, so we stopped believing ourselves. We began to think ourselves mad. We were diagnosed as mentally ill, riddled with psychosomatic nonsense, difficult, and our own testimony about how we felt and acted was deemed unreliable. The sound and the fury, signifying nothing.

We tried to cover it all up, to appear as normal as possible. Sometimes it worked, sometimes we couldn't keep a lid on it. Then something clicked. We realised something else was wrong, that there was a diagnosis that actually did apply to us, and set out to get that verified externally so we would be believed.

That was harder than we thought.

Asperger Syndrome is the name commonly given to a form of autism. It is a lifelong neurological disability that affects how people see the world, process information and relate to others.

It affects social communication, social interaction and social imagination. So, how we communicate with others, how we interact with others, how we predict (or rather can't) others' behaviour - which can be mistaken for a lack of empathy. There are other associated characteristics, like intense special interests, sensory processing problems, anxiety and difficulty with changes to routines.

There are positive attributes too, like harnessing those special interests for focus and attention to detail, and a rare kind of honesty when directly questioned.

It has long been accepted that is is more difficult to diagnose women and girls with autism. There are stereotypes to overcome, including within the medical profession, partly due to most of the literature discussing males and most research looking for male autistic participants. Simon Baron-Cohen's theory of the extreme male brain is increasingly popular. The typical special interests of autistic girls are more socially acceptable - animals, fashion, pop music - and women are socialised to be kind and forced into playing well with others, whereas 'boys will be boys'.

The difficulty with being subjected to this situation is the enormous amount of negative reinforcement that needs to be fought against in order to break free of it. Bullying and other sources of difficulty lay a foundation which causes us to constantly call the authenticity of our lived experiences into question, and the appropriation of diagnostic tools such as the Autism Quotient as memes by some online communities only further serves to trivialize the difficulties being faced.

Everyone's a little bit autistic.

I'm making something out of nothing, everyone does that.

Without appropriate support, this cycle and constant questioning can continue indefinitely. Even after an individual is screened or diagnosed, this mode of thinking often persists: 'No-one noticed any of this for thirty years, so how can I trust in this label?'

Ironically, it is the years of conditioning brought about by living our lives as a neurological minority which paint us into this corner: we learn to suppress certain behaviors in order to 'pass' as best we can, as a means to get by and meet the expectations of the world around us. As a result, symptoms become masked and may go unnoticed. For example, kicking one's legs or sitting on one's hands stands out less than rocking, but still stems from the same need. Flicking fingers are shoved into coat pockets; the lining may quickly wear out and become destroyed, but that is a small price to pay when no other options seem available. These are but a few examples of dysfunctional coping strategies which only serve to exhaust an individual.

Where we're going to

There are many reasons for obtaining a diagnosis, and some use the label for practical reasons without accepting disability as part of their selves. As Campbell (2009, p. 27) says,

> Without a classification or diagnosis it is very difficult to have certain needs arising out of bodily or mental differences recognised … the processes of identity formation *cannot be* separated from the individual who is brought into being through those very subjectifying processes.

Personally, I (Penny) needed the diagnosis to understand myself and stop punishing myself, to accept myself as disabled and know how to work around it. The benefits of reasonable adjustments and so on came later, but I was very aware that the choice of whether or not to pursue a formal diagnosis, and whether that diagnosis would be NHS or privately obtained, would not just impact on my feelings of legitimacy but also on how my disability would be viewed by educational institutions, funders, employers and so on. All kinds of people apply conditions to disability, for reasons of bureaucracy and prejudice but also to obtain some kind of critical perspective on what it means. Is this person authentically impaired? They need written evidence plus the equivalent of peer review or an impact factor to make that judgement.

For me (Mari), the primary impetus was my love of my job. My role is very focused around metadata management, so skills such as my attention to detail and ability to systemize and organize information into logical hierarchies are a natural fit, and I find the work very rewarding. The problem is that until early last year I was fighting what felt like a losing battle against migraines, nosebleeds, constant fatigue and low-grade fevers/infections. These were clearly the symptoms of stress, but I couldn't pinpoint their source: I liked my job. It was Penny who initially suggested the possibility that I might have Asperger Syndrome, and as she has known me well for some time, I took her opinion very seriously. As I researched, I began to see intimately familiar experiences (which I had never shared with anyone) being described, which was a very surreal experience for me.

From a more practical standpoint, I also saw the possibility for reasonable accommodations to be made for me at work. I was beginning to find names for pain I had no idea how to describe (or simply thought everyone else experienced but was better at tolerating than me). My difficulty with high-pitched monitor whines was no longer being 'too sensitive' but rather 'sensory processing disorder'. My tendency to hear words spoken to me as garbled at times wasn't my being inattentive, but rather 'auditory processing delay'.

'Overload' by Mari

[Please watch the video: http://vimeo.com/52193530#]

Many of the accommodations I needed were fairly simple and possible within the scope of my role: noise isolating headphones, written rather than verbal instructions, the opportunity to telecommute occasionally to recuperate, doodling in meetings (which helps me focus on conversation). Obtaining these accommodations was my most immediate goal when I began on this journey; I did not wish to feel as if was being forced to choose between my job and my health. After years of doubting my sensory perceptions, the terminology I was coming across in my research, and the specificity with which the symptoms were outlined, finally made me feel as if my pain was being given a degree of legitimacy. This gave me the courage and emotional reserves to pursue a diagnosis in earnest.

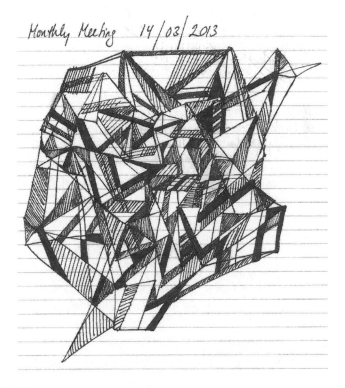

Doodle by Mari

My experience has, in some ways, been the reverse of Penny's. Although my journey began out of an immediate concern over my employment, I have found myself significantly re-evaluating my sense of self throughout this process.

As my screening and diagnosis have been extremely recent (six months and a week ago, respectively), I am still very much in the midst of coming to terms with my identity as a disabled person, and what that means.

The first stop on the journey

Both of us came to the idea of being autistic via female friends, rather than medical professionals or mental health services. Fictional and media representations of autistic people came later. Penny had read the experiences of her friend K, who had detailed the process of seeking and obtaining a diagnosis on LiveJournal, and Mari's journey began via a suggestion from Penny.

It's true that once you know a lot about autism, you start seeing it everywhere. Not the 'everyone is on the spectrum' thing, as the spectrum is just a way of explaining the range of abilities people with autism have; it is not like the Kinsey scale. However, you begin to recognise the signs in other people, and I (**Penny**) started to notice it in myself and later in Mari.

Seeing myself in K's accounts frightened and excited me simultaneously. I felt like a hypochondriac, the sort of person who puts generic symptoms into a search engine and comes out with 87 different possible life-threatening illnesses. My information literacy and critical thinking skills made me doubt myself intensely with this new possibility, but my curious mind meant I sought every kind of information going and then proceeded to assess, collate and discard whatever I found. My access to subscription resources via the Open University, where I was a student at the time, and my ability to understand and work with those sources, was invaluable. There is a lot of quackery and misinformation around autism.

I usually find it very difficult to see myself in others' accounts of themselves, which I later learned is fairly typical of autistic people, but what K wrote made sense to me in a way that the endless accounts written by non-autistic people about their child or sibling scattered across the media never did.

I think the final thing to click was K's experiences with gender, which mirrored my own, and I ended up discussing this in detail during my diagnostic assessment.

Watch comic strip: story, Penny and artist Steve Horry

I came to the understanding that few 'phases' of my growing-up were just passing fancy; rather, all were ways of trying to understand and cope with the messages I was receiving about the world. My dislike of certain textures was not fussiness but sensory overload I was unable to suppress. I tried to make the world logical. Girls are not like this, therefore I am not a girl. I like this person, therefore I must dress like them even if it does not suit me. I tried to learn the rules and be normal, and consistently got it wrong, as people are not consistent and do not constantly analyse the world the way I do. I began to understand this, through reading both personal accounts and journal articles. I also began to understand why I did not like uncertainty, why I checked my watch and panicked constantly if my husband was late home, why I got so upset if plans had to change. I was not throwing a tantrum.

I (Mari) had spent a great deal of time researching for several months, and was voracious as Penny in doing so. This was time well spent, as it intellectually armed me with a specific array of information, which I would eventually bring to my GP (and later, my caseworker with the

National Autistic Society). However, for me, there was still very much a disconnect between intellectual and emotional acceptance of the possibility that I might be autistic, and until this gap was bridged I found it very difficult to vocalize my concerns with a medical professional. My concerns were not unfounded: I had once tried to describe my experiences of synaesthesia and my constant need to move/fidget to a counsellor while at university in order to try and make sense of them, only to have those concerns dismissed as 'trying to be different' and 'just nerves' respectively.

Like Penny, my experience was riddled with self-doubt. My husband said that at the rate and thoroughness with which I was researching the symptoms of various mental illnesses (including hypochondria itself!), we should just buy a copy of the DSM. Later on, my support worker would repeatedly point out that my autistic traits were incredibly obvious, including my insistence on asking her specifically what she meant every time she said that.

In other words, my need to research, evaluate and assess autism only proved my autism further.

'Information seeking' in any form is a matter of associating one concept with another. As autistics, the associations we form are seen as unusual and thus often misunderstood -- but this does not invalidate their worth. A critical advantage offered by dialogue, community and conversation in online spaces is that it does not need to be limited to verbal (or even written) formats.The 'missing link' which allowed me to explore the idea of being diagnosed and receiving support was not an article or text, but rather a response to a sound clip I sent to Penny.

Music and sound are a tactile/kinesthetic as well as auditory experience for me, and I have a tendency to listen to certain things (often repeatedly) in order to calm myself down. I sent this clip to her as an example, and in return she sent me a YouTube link to a song which evoked the same sensory response, despite objectively sounding very different to the original clip. Penny was able to understand the sensory association immediately, with no need for verbal explanation. Being able to communicate effortlessly through my 'native language' was a key moment of validation which provided a buffer against the transactional costs of seeking help early on.

'Lamp sound' by Mari

[Please listen to: https://soundcloud.com/allthethings-1/nightelfstreetlamp]

[Please watch the YouTube video:
http://innovativelibraries.org.uk/il/stars]

Travelling in parallel

Mari: I am aware that while I have faced many obstacles along this journey, I have also been afforded a great deal of privilege in my life that mitigates many other difficulties I could have encountered. This is precisely the problem; often the most critical and useful information is inaccessible - financially or otherwise. In addition, I had understanding, compassionate medical professionals who listened to me and my concerns - many other women do exactly the same only to have their concerns dismissed. I was well aware that the research I carried out and the information I gathered would not guarantee a diagnosis itself, but the reassurance it provided on this journey has been invaluable.

Penny: I wonder how different my life would have been if I hadn't been considered clever and if I hadn't been so tenacious and persistent. I could read, write, pass exams and sometimes shut up. That got me through school, in the end, but not through university the first two times. Had I been less academically promising, and less able to copy non-autistic people for short periods to get by, would I have been diagnosed earlier? Perhaps not, given the era and my gender, and my education meant I could understand the process later. It also meant I could navigate my way through some areas of my life as though I was not disabled, even though this was exhausting, and when I was asked to provide a list of reasonable adjustments for work with no guidelines whatsoever, I was able to research and articulate the help I may need.

We understand the internet, we understand information, we understand academic papers and monographs and we understand blogging and social media. These things helped us in our journeys, but we know we are lucky.

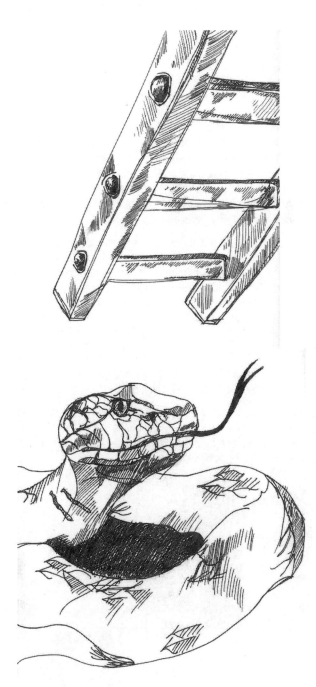

Snake and ladder sketches by Mari

Just the beginning

Diagnosis is very recent and raw for Mari. I (**Penny**) am two years in at the time of writing, so feel I can describe the process for you.

I am sent a developmental questionnaire about my childhood and adolescence, to pass on to a parent or someone who knew me well when I was younger. I post this to my mother, with instructions to send it directly to the clinic. On the day, I am encouraged to bring my husband and mum, so the psychologist can ask them more questions and also so they can be there when I receive my diagnosis. This is not just to support me, but so that they understand why it has been made.

In the weeks before the appointment, I do not sleep and constantly feel sick. I fear being told I am a fraud. I am myself suspicious of people on the autism forums I visit online who have proudly diagnosed themselves. Some have found the diagnostic process too long and difficult and pulled out, some have been rejected for assessment referrals by their GPs and psychiatrists, some do not seek medical confirmation at all. I am certain that I want an official diagnosis, on the NHS, even if I was able to go private - which I am not able to afford. I want to trust in the label and know that I (and my money) have no influence on its application.

My GP reassures me that if it is not Asperger Syndrome, it is not nothing, and I will not be sent home with a flea in my ear. I still feel sick.

I get to the clinic, and the psychologist tells me the appointment will take two hours. I am distracted early on by the cockeyed radiator cover behind her. I tell her this, worrying, and that I am sorry for looking past her head rather than into her eyes, and she smiles. I know it is going to be okay.

Radiator comic strip: story, Penny and artist Steve Horry

She asks me many questions about childhood, university, dropping out, work, my life now, why I seek a diagnosis (quality of life, mainly). Half an hour before the end, she calls my husband and mother into the room, and asks them some more questions, including how my husband and I met, how our marriage is going etc. It is all intimate and scary. Finally, the psychologist says she has no doubt in her mind and that I have Asperger Syndrome. I nearly cry with relief.

She hands me a brown envelope with a leaflet about the NAS, a list of books to read and a sheet about the Autism Act 2010, which says I am entitled to a social services assessment. I later look on my council's website and find that the assessment I am entitled to, as everyone is, but help I am not as I do not meet the criteria.

A few weeks later I am sent a one-page letter I can use when people need proof of my diagnosis, and a full diagnostic report. A copy is sent to my GP and my psychiatrist, who sees me one last time to check I am OK. The last part of the report tells me that I should focus on the positives of my condition. I finally start to believe in the diagnosis.

Gone exploring

Misdiagnosis is not uncommon for individuals in situations like ours, as we lack a vocabulary or frame of reference to adequately articulate what we experience. Yes, you are reading these words before you on this page, but like so much else, our capacity to string these sentences together is reliant on our mastery of systemizing and pattern-matching. So much of what we experience cannot be expressed through words.

Naturally, this inability to fully describe how we relate to the world can make childhood a bewildering experience. Attempts at 'translating' are often rebuffed, even though no malice is involved: 'No, the television is on mute, it isn't making any noise'. Time spent in school becomes terrifying, each day filled with sentences like 'Days don't have colors, you [slur],' or fears that you will be hit, spat on or have your possessions taken by your peers.

When something as basic as your sensory input is repeatedly called into question, the result is a profound lack of understanding of one's own identity. This can result in anxiety and depression, which can significantly impact quality of life.

Attempts to make sense of these difficulties within a clinical context can also result in incorrect and possibly damaging diagnoses. For example, certain types of repetitive behavior (which are a key part of the autistic profile) can often be misattributed to conditions such as obsessive-compulsive disorder by an uninformed professional. This pathologizing of characteristics which are not necessarily harmful to the individual also severely impairs the sense of self.

The autistic activist known as ArecBalrin wrote in the comments of a June 2013 Guardian article that often we are not able to articulate our experiences because we are not approached in the right way. Teenager Naoki Higashida uses a Q&A format in part of his book, recently translated by David Mitchell, and Balrin says:

> It might not occur to him yet that there is something wrong with the questions and that he can challenge some of the assumptions implicit in them.

One of the assumptions is that the autistic perspective or response is always defective, when often it is logical and people of the neurotypical phenotype are the ones acting illogically.

It is considered rude in many situations to say what you mean and mean what you say - socially, we are supposed to dance around issues. Someone you know spills your coffee at work. They offer to pay for a replacement. The general understanding for many neurotypical people is that the offer is in itself the reparation for the damage caused, and the expectation in most contexts is that you will smile and tell them not to worry about it. All of this is subtext. Logically, the person who spills the drink should not make an offer if they hope it will not be accepted, and the person whose drink was spilled should not say it does not matter if they were really looking forward to that drink. Of course, these 'rules' are not hard and fast, because everything in the non-autistic world is ambiguous; so as soon as you learn one thing is true, then something contradicts it.

Much like English grammar.

Timelines

Penny

January 2010: Read post on LiveJournal from K about how she might have Asperger Syndrome, and why she thinks that. I have heard of it before, but usually only in the context of children and teenagers or of adult males who live with their mothers. What she says rings a bell, and we are very similar in some ways. I start frantically reading up on the subject and watching every TV programme and movie I can find on the subject. I read endless blogs and lurk on forums set up for people with autism and their families. I go through the Autism tag on the Guardian online and read every piece for the past five years.

February 2010: Read post on LiveJournal from K saying that she has actually been diagnosed with AS. I make a list of everything from my childhood onwards that may be relevant, behaviours and experiences, and make an appointment with my new GP. He tells me he can only think of one or two local psychiatrists who believe in adult Asperger's diagnosis, but agrees to a referral.

March 2010: Read a link from K to a 2008 article in the National Autistic Society magazine, then called *Communication*, by Dale Yaull-Smith. The paragraph that resonated with K most also hit me like an electric shock:

> I often wondered why I found areas of my life, such as planning, decision-making, motivation and styles of thinking, so difficult while others appeared to deal with these areas of life with ease. I observed people and tried to copy some physical behaviours e.g. body language which I have found exhausting because, with hindsight, I know that my concentration has been fundamentally focused on trying to understand and interpret other people's behaviours and intentions. As a result, I managed to get by on a superficial level but never really grasped functioning socially on a deeper level. (Yaull-Smith, 2008)

October 2010: First of three appointments with a psychiatrist, the only person who can refer me to the tertiary diagnostic service at Sheffield and apply to the primary care trust for the funding to go to another area for diagnosis. I have to chase this funding decision up, so does he.

April 2011: I read an interview with Paddy Considine in the Telegraph, where he explains that his Asperger's diagnosis was a relief. He is a performer, I am a performer. It helps to know that someone I admire enormously has this, was diagnosed late and approaches performance in a similar way. Later he is interviewed for radio, and I love him even more.

[Please watch YouTube video:
http://innovativelibraries.org.uk/paddy]

May 2011: Diagnosis.

July 2011: Participant in autism research at University of Sheffield, where I am told that I am in the top 5% for the verbal reasoning, pattern matching and other intelligence-measuring tasks the researchers gave me, but 'obviously autistic' in the social and storytelling tasks. I was reminded of the storytelling task in October 2012, when asked to play an information literacy game with story cubes in Andrew Walsh's games in libraries session at Library Camp. I couldn't do that, either - my reading of the abstract objects was too literal.

November 2011: Apply for, and am accepted for, a position as Ambassador for the National Autistic Society. I go on to appear in the national and local media multiple times, help launch an employment campaign at the House of Commons, work with my local council on issues affecting adults with autism and be invited to Downing Street in recognition of my advocacy work.

[http://www.guardian.co.uk/society/video/2013/mar/08/disability-workplace-autism-video]

[Please watch YouTube video:
http://innovativelibraries.org.uk/AutWork]

July 2012: Try to get support from the Open University in my final degree project. Staff are part-time and hard to contact. Academic staff refuse to change any criteria. Tutor accuses me of blackmailing him when I ask for assistance to fulfil my potential. It takes 7 weeks to get any help. Two weeks before the deadline I finally see a support worker, who only knows how to work with dyslexic and low ability students. In December, I will find out that my marks actually went down from the pre-support draft report mark, denying me a First in my degree by a whisker.

August 2012: Begin my first job (fixed-term contract) in a library, which is also my first job with reasonable adjustments in place. By Christmas I learn how to thrive in the right working environment.

January 2013: Watch the Temple Grandin HBO movie on Sky. Freaked out by the scene in the cafeteria - the director has shown exactly how it feels to be overwhelmed by sensory stimuli, and elsewhere in the film why autistic meltdowns happen.

June 2013: Read Guardian feature with David Mitchell and Naoki Higashida. Higashida sets more neurons firing in my brain with this on why he repeats questions and actions, which rings so true for me:

> I imagine a normal person's memory is arranged continuously, like a line. My memory, however, is more like a pool of dots. I'm always 'picking up' these dots – by asking my questions – so I can arrive back at the memory that the dots represent.
> (Higashida, 2013)

Diagnosis is not the end, it is only the beginning of understanding. I have never been able to articulate what Higashida says so beautifully, but I experience it all the time.

Mari

September 2011: Period of illness at work which does not seem to improve. Suggestion from Penny to consider Asperger Syndrome. She and I would engage in several conversations on the topic via e-mail and Twitter over the course of the next 22 months throughout the course of the journey.

November 2011: *Newsround: My Autism & Me* transmits on CBBC. The segment, which was presented by a young girl with Asperger Syndrome, was geared towards a younger audience, but information was presented in such a clear and straightforward way that I found it difficult to ignore. Additionally, while I saw a great deal of my younger self in Rosie (the presenter) it was actually footage of her younger brother (who is nonverbal) engaging in various repetitive behaviors which really drove the point home. I had to leave the room because his actions were too overwhelming to watch at times.

'Newsround stress' by Mari

[Please watch YouTube video: http://innovativelibraries.org.uk/AutMe]

December 2011: Read Attwood book, photocopy and highlight relevant pages. Research his work further, and study his website. Literally gasp and drop my iPad at this paragraph when I see it, and begin to cry:

> Some girls may not seek integration but escape into imagination. If you are not successful with your peers, you can try to find an alternative world where you are valued and appreciated. The girl may identify with a fictional character such as Harry Potter or Hermione Granger, who faces adversity but has special powers and friends. If she feels lonely, then imaginary friends can provide companionship, support and comfort. There can be an interest in ancient civilizations to find an old world in which you would feel at home, or another country such as Japan where you would be accepted and of like mind or even another planet with an interest in science fiction or a special and intense interest in the traditional fantasy worlds of witches, fairies and mythology. (2011, Online)

I'm an avid fan of Tolkien and many other fantasy intellctual properties/franchises, have the equivalent of a first degree in Latin, and have been an Anglophile since the age of eleven. My dream as a child was to move to the UK - and so I did. Needless to say, this paragraph had a profound effect on me.

January 2012: Printed and highlighted relevant sections from NAS website to take to GP appointment.

Feb 2012: 1st GP visit. GP took my concerns seriously based on the thoroughness of the information I had presented (see previous two points), though suggested it might be 'just anxiety'. In the time leading up to this appointment, I felt as if I had to do homework in order to present my case.

Aug 2012: No word on referral. Visited GP again, who was very upset on my behalf. It appeared that my case had been lost in bureaucracy, as I needed a referral outside of my local NHS area. Both my GP and I wrote letters to the relevant parties to speed along my referral, and my GP had me fill out a quality of life questionnaire from the World Health Organization to augment my case.

Nov 2012: Referral letter received for a screening by the National Autistic Society. I was required to fill out two multiple-choice questionnaires and answer a list of questions in preparation for this screening. I was also given a short form for my parents to fill out.

Jan 2013: Screened. NAS support worker determines I would benefit from the services of their ASSIST programme. Appointments with a support worker recur once or twice a month and are ongoing. Am told it will likely be 6-10 months before I receive word on an NHS referral. Reasonable accommodations are made at work; quality of life significantly improves.

April 2013: Am told NHS referrals are taking upwards of a year, and am encouraged to seek a private diagnosis for 'peace of mind'. Earliest appointment available privately within reasonable traveling distance is mid-June.

June 2013: Diagnosis.

Where we're at

Mari: As stated, I've just been recently officially diagnosed, so many of the raw feelings I felt when I was screened in January have returned to the surface. My goals as I work through these feelings as they relate to my identity are twofold - the first is to process and come to terms with what that diagnosis means, and I expect to some extent that is a task I will be continually working on. This healing process is yet another phase in which my information literacy skills will be critical.

The second goal I have is very similar to one that Penny first shared with me when I began on this journey, and is why I have chosen to speak out about my experiences:

I want to help prevent others from suffering as I have.

Penny's and my journeys highlight what an arduous process this has been, and it should not be the norm. My support worker has suggested becoming involved with her advocacy work once my diagnosis and the emotions surrounding it are a little less immediate, and this is something I absolutely intend to do. In doing so, I will be using much of the same skillset I harnessed while developing information literacy classes in my first job as an academic liaison librarian. After all, both stem from a desire to make knowledge more accessible, in every sense of the word.

Penny: I am about to return to 'brick university' education, hopefully this time successfully after completing my OU degree, and I am petrified that the disability support will not work out. I have loved my job this year, and know now what it is like to work with adjustments in place, and how my condition can actually help me in information work. I will be studying for an MSc in Digital Library Management.

I have become even more determined to be a good ambassador for the NAS and women with autism, and to have more than my disabilities (autism, cerebral palsy and dyspraxia) in my life, despite my activism. I think I make a better role model if I work in a 'normal' job and have interests outside of autism, such as my newly-found love of sprinting, but I still want to change the situation so that other women do not have to become librarians and fighters in order to seek information and diagnosis and find self-acceptance.

Selected Bibliography

Attwood, T (2008). *The Complete Guide to Asperger's Syndrome.*London: Jessica Kingsley Publishers.

Attwood, T (2011) 'Girls and Women Who Have Asperger's Syndrome' [online] available from: http://www.tonyattwood.com.au/index.php/about-aspergers/girls-and-women-who-have-aspergers (Accessed 18 July 2013)

Campbell, FK (2009). *Contours of Ableism: The production of Disability and Abledness*. Basingstoke: Palgrave Macmillan. 26-27.

Mitchell, D & Higashida, N (2013). 'David Mitchell: learning to live with my son's autism', *The Guardian* [online]. 29 June 2013. Available from: http://www.guardian.co.uk/society/2013/jun/29/david-mitchell-my-sons-autism (Accessed: 29 June 2013)

Spicer, D (1998). Autistic and Undiagnosed: My Cautionary Tale. In: *Asperger Syndrome Conference*, March 12-13 1998, Västerås, Sweden.

Turkle, S (1997). *Life on the Screen: Identity in the Age of the Internet*. London: Phoenix. 180, 256, 318.

Yaull-Smith, D (2008). 'Girls on the spectrum', *Communication*, Spring 2008. 30-31.

The Stable Group / David Mathew

This paper is a reflective account of a challenge that the author
undertook, years earlier, as part of his M.A. in Psychoanalytic Studies.
Given that the challenge at the time was itself a reflective task, this
paper might be considered a reflection of a reflection. As part of his
M.A. the author had to observe group dynamics in a work setting for
ten weeks and present not only his report of what he saw and felt at the
time of the observation, but also an interpretation of the report, as
viewed through the lens of psychoanalytic theory. One further step on
from that earlier material, this paper reflects on those previous
reflections and interpretations, and questions some of the author's
assumptions of the time. By challenging his earlier self in this way, the
author also reflects on what a psychoanalytic exploration of the
workers at a horse stable might tell us about our relationship with our
learners.

Introduction

Although much of my work is in the fields of education,
psychoanalysis or writing, I was once duty-bound to conduct a weekly
observation of the staff working at a stable for horses, for ten
consecutive weeks. The reason for this is that I was working my way
through a Masters in Psychoanalytic Studies and one of the modules
dealt with institutional observations. The members of the class were
each asked to choose a profession that they had no connection to -
either professionally nor as a hobby - and to try to arrange a time and a
day of the week that they could visit a group of people that met at this

time and on this day regularly. While some of my classmates chose to approach (for example) banks or council offices, with a view to sitting in on team meetings for week after week, I doubted that this would be interesting to me, and I decided to attempt a group observation that might have the pleasurable by-product of getting me out into the fresh air for a couple of hours per week.

Approximately a twenty-minute walk from where I lived was a working stable for horses. One day I took a walk up the hill, where I was greeted warmly at the stable door by the woman who ran the stable; for the purposes of my weekly reports I changed her name to Ellie, and although the prospect of my visit on a weekly basis had no advantage for her or for her team, she agreed to my proposal after I'd explained that I was only there to watch and not get in the way.

For the purposes of this paper I have chosen extracts from two of the total-recall observation reports that I wrote at the time (my first visit and my eighth visit), and I have included edited commentaries on the same. By necessity the extracts contain people's names, but all of these names have been anonymised, and where a name appears for the first time I have included a brief description of that person's role in parentheses.

Extract from Observation 1: Visit 1: 'Here there is no weather ...'

As I approached the main building, the noise from the horses beyond was very loud. The horses were neighing and calling. At the door I paused and listened to them and heard them kicking their stable doors. I knocked on the front door and waited, standing in the rain and regarding the sign on the door that warned me that German Shepherd dogs patrolled the premises.

Ellie opened the door. She was on her own, not holding a dog. She said 'Hi!' and shook my hand. I was let in and I entered the building through a hallway that leads past where the dogs usually sleep. 'Don't worry,' Ellie told me, 'the dogs are up in one of the pastures with Rob [Ellie's husband]. They like to follow him about when he's on his tractor. You won't meet them. And even if you do, if you stay near me, that's a sign of approval for them. Means you're accepted.'

The other side of the main stable building is open to the weather but is roofed. It was under this roof that I conducted my observation. As I moved into the noise and the surprising warmth of the stable, a few of the women present nodded at me or smiled. Mrs N (horse-owner, volunteer worker) and Steph (worker) groomed a large white horse in the open space. Jasper (handyman) filled a bucket from a nearby tap.

Jasper walked out the back, swaggering slightly. Beyond the main stable building and the two other smaller stables, I saw a large barn. Its door was open wide, and I could see buckets, bags of horse food, ropes, harnesses, and tins of what turned out to be saddle care products. Jasper headed in the direction of this open door.

Lou (a worker) left this barn and walked towards us, carrying a bucket of food. 'This is X, everybody!' Ellie called out (meaning me). Lou said, 'Hi there. I promise to be on my best behaviour.' She walked towards a stall with a sign on the door that read SNOOPY. Inside the stall, a large horse kicked at the door. 'All right, all right, I'm coming. Hold your horses!' And she laughed loudly.

'The old ones are the best, eh, X?' Ellie whispered to me.

I smiled and nodded and returned the greetings of Terry (handyman), who was sweeping hay, straw and manure from a stable into a tidy pile.

Ellie said, 'Rob's in top field. Ms J [worker] and Miss V [horse-owner] are bringing in the rest [of the horses]. They won't be too long, I shouldn't think.'

While we listened to the horses screaming for their food and water and kicking at their doors, Jasper returned, carrying a stool. 'Sit anywhere you like,' said Ellie. 'But you'll probably see best if you're there.' She pointed at a point on the threshold between the main stable and the open air. Jasper said, 'Here you go, mate,' and handed me the stool.

There were fourteen stalls in total: ten in the main building, four in two separate buildings out the back, all within view. All fourteen stalls were occupied.

Ellie said, 'Terry: could you see to the north fence, please?

Terry looked disappointed by the request, but he leaned his broom against the wall and abandoned his pile of straw and manure. 'See you in a bit,' he said to me. 'Have fun.'

The workers continued with their tasks: combining their work about the yard and stable (cleaning, sweeping) with their care for the animals.

Ellie sent Jasper out to take a look at one of the fences that had been damaged in the dog-pen which had been built for Zack and Puppy but into which they hadn't moved yet. Jasper sighed but did not argue. He picked up a hammer and a jar of nails that were on the floor near one of the stalls.

Ms J and Miss V returned to the stable, each holding a horse on a rein. The horses walked quickly and Ms J and Miss V had to stride to keep up.

Jasper told me that he was going to give Mrs N and Miss V 'a lesson' – they had only recently moved their horses to this particular stable. He began his talk by explaining that everyone had their own storage space in the barn. Meanwhile, Ms J started to fill up the first in a long line of buckets with water. Miss V began combing and brushing some of the worst of the mud out of the horses' hair, one by one, with the horses tied loosely to fittings on the walls; the horses were allowed to dip their heads in order to eat from large plastic bowls of dry feed. There was little conversation apart from Jasper's voice; everyone was busy and the operation was extremely streamlined, with everyone present well aware of what needed to be done. Ellie swept up the pile of straw and droppings that Terry had left behind when he went away to fix the fence.

Ellie then strode out into the rain and walked to the other side of an enormous pile of horse droppings, out of my line of sight. On the way she deposited what she had just swept up. The other workers worked efficiently in her temporary absence. Buckets were filled; bowls were filled with different amounts of different kinds of food (in the barn) and the bowls were brought back so that every horse was fed in turn. All of the women took turns at the taps, filling buckets and then pushing the hose into the next bucket when they were finished. The horses accepted their interim gifts of carrots and sweet pellets with good grace, but what they wanted were the bowls of food, which looked like a cross between wet cement and porridge. Such conversation as took place was deceptively cursory – almost rude – to one another; the workers went about their business, doing what needed to be done before it got any darker.

Gradually the horses, as they were fed, became quieter and got on with the business of eating, which required their full concentration. Some were given football-sized plastic toys half-filled with a different kind of edible pellet (for mental stimulation). The horses were treated with love, attention, kindness – and the tasks the workers were involved in were set to with a mixture of enthusiasm and can-do. Ms J swept the floor and carried dustpans of wet straw and manure to the dung-heap outside. Steph turned off the tap once she had checked that all of the buckets by the wall were full. Then she took the buckets, one by one, to the stalls for the horses. Jasper led Mrs N and Miss V out beyond the storage barn, where I could see an even bigger barn.

When Ellie returned she rubbed rain from her hair and stamped her boots. As I was preparing to leave I thought I might offer a simple observation. 'It can't be nice to work in these conditions,' I said, indicating the downpour. She replied, 'Here there is no weather. Horses have to be fed. There's no weather.'

I told her that my time was up and that I had to go. 'I hope you found it useful,' she said, and I answered that I had indeed and that I'd see her next week. I called goodbye, and Ms J, Steph and Lou (who was standing in a stall, watching Snoopy eat) all said goodbye to me and waved.

As I left the main building, stepping out into the rain, I heard the dogs barking somewhere behind me. I walked down the drive, and not knowing whether or not to close the open gate behind me, I left it open.

Original Commentary on Observation 1

I felt nervous on my approach to the stable: much more so than I had on the evening when I had walked there on spec to ask for permission to observe. My anxiety, I am sure, had much to do with the fact that I had never been further than the main door and that I had little idea of what I would find beyond the door. In essence, I arrived at a ramshackle building, where all I could see were fences and paddocks (at that time unoccupied); not a single person was visible, as they were all 'behind the scenes' working. Added to this was my apprehension around barking dogs.

I was warmly received, which was a relief. Not only did I not appear threatening to the group, there were even obvious attempts to make me like individual members of it. For example, when Ellie whispered that the old jokes were the best (sarcastically), she was mocking one of her team but simultaneously attempting to get me on her side. Similarly, the use of the word 'mate' to me throughout was an attempt at bonding. The fact that I was offered a stool to sit on made me feel welcomed as an observer. I formed the impression that Ellie and her team were happy for me to be there – proud to show off their work, in fact – and the general sense of good-natured humour, despite the weather conditions, helped enforce this.

If the primary task (Bion, 1961) was to look after horses (their feeding, their grooming, the cleaning of their environment), I would say that this task was adhered to with professional aplomb, and achieved. With the single exception of an unvoiced complaint from Terry when he was asked to abandon one chore (sweeping) in order to take on another (fixing a fence in the rain, nursing a bad arm as he did), the group undertook their jobs with grit and determination. There appeared to be no hierarchy of tasks or of personnel: everyone was there to get the jobs done so that they could all go home. This made me impressed with Ellie as a leader: she has built a solid group, no doubt strengthened by the fact that she is 'hands-on' as well and does not only issue orders. I believe that it is largely because of Ellie that the group maintained and maintains its stability: having established herself as a good leader, Ellie is able to request supplementary tasks of her team (e.g. fixing the fence, or even fetching the stool) as means of reducing and containing group anxiety.

My presence did not have an obvious effect on the work rate of the group. The workers were friendly to me, and it is possible that Ellie and Terry (in particular) were attempting to curry my favour; then again, perhaps this is the way they are with every visitor. There was an absence of competitiveness among the group, and no sense of female rivalry. There was no sense of their waiting for me to leave; on the contrary, I gained the impression that they would have been content for me to have stayed until the stable was completely clean and tidy. Cleanliness and tidiness would have equated to the primary task having been fully achieved.

Look at the surface, I jotted down in my notebook on my return home. What is under? Look at boundaries: the electric fences. They are to keep intruders out, but also to keep the horses in; they are the boundaries of the container. Each paddock is a sub-container. And then I underlined a question that I hoped to answer in the following weeks of my observation:

In the absence of palpable tension or anxiety, can this absence itself create and brew up tension and anxiety? I thought of the novel (Ballard 1988) in which the children of rich parents, stifled by too much love and 'idyllic' surroundings (a state-of-the-art walled compound) go on a murderous campaign and kill their caregivers. And while I knew that this was exaggerating anything that would ever occur at the stable, there remained some comparisons. Not only is the work group containing its own anxiety; it is also obliged to contain the anxiety of the horses so that they do not spook.

A horse's anxiety is contagious: it spreads to the whole herd. A horse can be spooked by the smell of blood, the smell of the vet; by a crisp packet blowing in the breeze across the bridle-path.

All of this must be contained by the working group.

Contemporary Response to Observation 1

Years have passed since I wrote this observation and my commentary on it, and although my circumstances have changed, my impressions of that time remain vivid. I look back on a happy time and I recall the positive feedback that the observation earned (we were obliged to read them aloud in class).

I remember being challenged on my use of pseudonyms, and in particular questioned on my system of first names versus 'Miss' or 'Mrs' plus the first letter of the surname. Reflective accounts are only as strong as one's memory, but if memory serves this choice was a simple way of distinguishing between those who worked at the stable (but did not own their own horses) and those who owned their own horses (and volunteered their labour). I believe that my naming structure was an attempt at conveying an (unconsciously experienced) sense of respect on the horse-owners. I wonder what this says about me.

Personnel notwithstanding, the stable is much the same as it was then. For the purposes of this article I made a return visit, and was surprised to be granted access: Ellie had stayed in the same position all of this time and she remembered me after a few seconds.

She asked me how my 'project' had gone, and I reminded her that I had visited once shortly after I knew I had passed my exams. Her eyes told me that she did not remember this visit, but it was a long time ago, so it is probably not surprising: I had visited the stable to say thank you one last time.

'Do you want to start watching us again?' Ellie asked. 'I don't think there's many you met last time. All fresh blood.'

For the last time I set foot into the stable. Two dogs barked, but they were different members of the team as well. The dogs I knew had long since passed away. These new dogs were no friendlier to casual visitors!

Entr'acte

The second observation that I will present was that of my eighth visit.

In the intervening weeks I had good reason to support my own views that Ellie had strong leadership qualities. '[I]t's very hard to describe what makes a really good manager,' says Isabel Menzies Lyth:

> There is … a lot of courage involved; you've got to be able to do things which, on the face of it, may seem unpopular, upset people … You are not kind all the time … Integrity is very important … the capacity for containment: [y]ou don't panic and

you are able to reflect and digest and think … The other thing about being a good leader is being a good example to the troops and sharing the hardships. (Pecotic 2002, pp.4-9)

Ellie had certainly had cause to share the hardships. Her beloved dog Puppy had been taken seriously ill (a brain tumour) and had had to be put down. Personally, I had become fond of Puppy, and to watch her physical decline over the two weeks preceding my eighth visit had been painful. No longer the bouncing, playful Puppy, she had become a clumsy burden to herself and to others. She frightened the horses (I think they sensed something of her condition) and she was apt to walk headfirst into gates that she must have seen as open even though they were closed.

The putting-down of Puppy had occurred a few days earlier. The surviving guard dog, Zack, had been introduced to a new partner – another puppy named Bonnie – and they had moved from the room by the stable's front door, to a shed with its own enclosed running area. Zack was teaching Bonnie how to fight and to bark with more aggression.

Two new horses had been moved in: a tiny Falabella and a regular-sized companion, which shared the same stall.

Ellie's young children – a boy and a girl – were in attendance for this following observation. It was the first time that I had seen the children.

Extract from Observation 2: Visit 8: 'There's always something sad around a stable...'

The horses were neighing and calling for their food, as is usual when I arrive on a Sunday. Some of the horses were kicking their stable doors. A few of the horses stuck their heads out of their stables to see who had come to see them but then they did not pay me much attention.

When I entered the yard, Miss V and Ellie immediately said hello to me and I returned the greeting, moving off into my corner where I usually watch from. I sat on my stool. I had not known it but I was to witness the instruction of one member of the team by another member of the team. Ms N was taking instruction from Ellie in the ways of easing the horse into having its hair clipped. In the meantime, Terry started to fill buckets with water from the tap.

Steph was preparing her horse to go out riding with Lou, to give the horses exercise, although this was late in the afternoon to take a horse out. She explained where they would be going – and also told everyone how long they thought they would be gone. 'Where's that tractor?' she asked rhetorically. Then she explained to me: 'The horses can't go where the tractor is because it's frightening to them and they spook. I won't be a second … ' By walking out to the gate with the horse tied up, Steph established where the tractor was and called back to Lou: 'It's fine, he's way out.' She then opened the gate and led her horse through.

Jasper arrived back at the stable, having been to collect the horse food for the week; he put it in the hay-barn and filled a couple of horses' hay-nets by strolling from stall to stall with a handful of hay each time.

Mrs N also moved almost wordlessly from stall to stall, beginning to put down straw, checking beds and removing droppings. She also changed the water in the buckets, carrying the buckets from the tap to each stall. She carried the droppings in a bucket out back to the dung heap.

The radio was on in an attempt to keep the horses quiet – but the main way of keeping a horse quiet is to invite it to eat, which Ms J and Mrs N were doing, filling buckets full of feed and water and distributing them around the various stalls of the stable. While Ellie instructed Ms N, Ellie's children walked into the stable, each of them carrying a broom that seemed huge next to their small bodies. Both of them looked at me on my stool and the boy said 'Hello' but the girl appeared shy and turned away.

Mrs N explained that the children were waiting for their father to come up the main drive and pick them up so that they could go on a tractor ride. She also told me that many of the horses had been inside all day, even though it was sunny, because Rob was fertilising the fields and killing weeds like ragwort because they're poisonous to the horses.

Ms J groomed the horses one by one as Ellie's lesson with Ms N continued. Ms J washed the horses' tail and feet; the horses are losing their winter coats and there was lots of hair everywhere. As Ms N and Ellie's lesson continued, Ms J picked the stones out of the horses' feet and polished their hooves. This all took place in the area directly outside the main stables.

For the purposes of the lesson, Ellie was carrying a switch (similar to a whip) which she has been using for several weeks to train the horse into not being frightened of the hair-clippers. She was teaching Ms N to hold an electric toothbrush and the switch in the same hand and to touch the switch gently over the horse's body, to get the horse used to the tickling sensation and the noise of the toothbrush's motor. She explained it to Ms N every step of the way: she explained that the clippers would be much louder for the horse and that this was the way to get her prepared.

'She has to get used to routine,' I overheard Ellie telling Ms N, tracing the switch underneath the horse's body, and in places where it might be tender. She kept talking to Ms N throughout the training, but as she explained, she was also talking to the horse, which occasionally swished its tail with dissatisfaction and stamped its back leg. When these signs of disappointment or discomfort arose, Ellie backed away, stopped for a while, and waited for the horse to calm down. Then she started again, keeping her voice level and calm at all times – trying not to spook the horse – and then repeating the process on both sides of the horse's body. 'The idea is to get the horse used to the noise and the feeling. Move the toothbrush nearer,' she instructed, while doing so to illustrate her point.

Shortly afterwards, Ellie started with the real clippers. In the meantime, Mrs N had been back to inform Ellie that there was a 'hot bale' in the feed barn. Ellie produced the horse clippers; they were the size of a brick. She turned them on and the horse quickly moved away from the loud noise. Immediately Ellie turned the clippers off and showed the horse the clippers, allowing the horse to sniff the clippers; then she tried again and said to Ms N, 'Give her a treat for being good.' Ms N fed the horse a spearmint pellet.

From where I sat I could just see the corner of the dogs' new home. The dogs continued to bark throughout my visit.

Suddenly Jasper started to laugh, somewhere outside the main barn, where the other stables house four horses. His laugh was booming. We all went towards the edge of the main barn to see what was going on, and there was the smallest horse imaginable, which I hadn't seen before now. It was a two and-a-half year-old Falabella (a miniature horse). The reason that Jasper was laughing was because the other horses are very nervous of the Falabella; they don't know how to treat her or react to her. Looking over their stable doors, one horse shied away from it as if afraid. Now, everybody laughed, and a discussion ensued about how the other horses were reacting. 'They don't know if it's a pony or a dog,' Jasper told me. The horse in question is about 2.5 feet tall to its shoulders.

From where I now stood, the dogs in their run could see me. Zack barked at me but was also apparently confused by the Falabella and started barking at the horse as well. Zack gradually became less aggressive as we remained in the area for a minute or two.

We returned to the main stable and I sat back down on my stool.

Ellie's lesson with Ms N came to an end. By this point Ms N was able to advance on her horse slowly with the switch and the toothbrush in the same hand; the horse was jumpy but it allowed Ms N to stroke her flanks and underbelly. 'Not even your hubby gets it so nice, I bet,' Ellie joked.

Ms N laughed.

Lou called from one of the stalls: 'Are you coming running on Tuesday night, Ellie?' Lou was doling out straw from a large flat plastic container: preparing a bed for the horse that would occupy the stall when it had been brought back from the fields shortly.

While Ellie's children continued to move their sweepings out to the dung-heap, the adults made plans for their evening of exercise. Lou, Ellie, Ms N, Ms J and Mrs N would all be participating.

'We all need to lose some weight,' Ms N confided in me.

'Speak for yourself!' said Ms J.

'So you're intending to arrive on time this week, Ellie?' said Lou.

The women had a laugh together – a semi-regular running session, weather permitting, which would also constitute both a team-bonding activity and a get-fit campaign in one. Last week Ellie had been late to join them.

'All right, all right,' Ellie said, acknowledging the chiding. 'Last one out, lock the doors,' she instructed. 'I'm off.'

'Me too,' I told her. 'Thanks as ever.'

When I left I was offered waves and goodbyes.

Original Commentary on Observation 2

'Management, if practised unimaginatively,' writes Anton Obholzer with Sarah Miller in 'Leadership, followership, and facilitating the creative workplace' (Huffington et al., 2004, p41), 'is leadership without the vision, and therefore, to a degree, the management and administration of the status quo.'

But when applied to the stable, can this view be squared? On the one hand, we might argue, Ellie is maintaining the status quo; but does this mean that she must also be an 'unimaginative' leader, as Obholzer suggests? I do not believe this is the case. The fact is that many of the tasks that mesh together for the group to achieve its primary task are repetitive; but this does not mean that her leadership style is without 'vision'. Indeed, I believe that an atmosphere has been created in which humour both bonds the group together and fends off group anxiety. In Obholzer's phrase, we might even regard the Stable as a 'creative workplace' – at least in the sense that anxiety seems contained and the primary task is achieved on a daily basis.

We might contend that the group at the Stable follows the theory that Freud posited in *Group Psychology and the Analysis of the Ego* (Freud 1922, Standard Edition 18, p116): that groups are 'a number of individuals who have put one and the same object in the place of their ego ideal and have consequently identified themselves with one another in their ego.' While it is probably true that the horses help to act as adhesives in the ego-integration of the group, I think this integration is also a result of Ellie's leadership.

In this eighth observation, Ellie showed further signs of being an authority – she was listened to by Ms N – but she did not show signs of being aloof in any way. Humbly, in fact, she accepted the jibes of the others when the subject of running came up: she became 'one of the girls' who had tried to shirk her exercise commitments in the past:

she effectively said sorry without saying sorry! But is this all that is present? In a paper entitled 'Some unconscious aspects of organizational life' (Obholzer and Roberts 1994, p11), William Halton offers an interesting interpretation of complaints: 'a staff group talking about their problems with the breakdown of the switchboard may at the same time be making an unconscious reference to a breakdown in interdepartmental communication. Or complaints about the distribution of car-park spaces may also be a symbolic communication about managers who have no room for staff concerns.' Given these remarks, perhaps we can dig deeper for a 'true' interpretation of the group's comments about Ellie's lateness when it comes to running. Perhaps they are unconsciously frustrated with her being slow to react to any number of other matters.

Returning to Obholzer, we read: '(M)anagers fall into states of increased bureaucracy, both "in the mind" and "in the system", and the managed fall into states of denigrating management. This can either take the form of casting managers as parasites who live off the work or creativity of the workers, or else for management not to be seen as real work... At an unconscious level the leader is perceived as giving the group a message: "I think I'm better than you are..." Leaders and managers are experienced as siblings who have reached "above their station." (p41)

It says much, I think, that this appears not to be the case at the Stable. There is unconscious recognition of the fact that although each member of the group knows his or her own roles at a basic level, more explicit task-giving, involving chores that deviate somewhat from the norm, is the responsibility of the leader. This is not challenged. Nor, however, do I believe that this behaviour should lead us to assume basic assumptions are in place. The Stable is work-focused; there is no sense of basic-assumption dependency...

As I have throughout the process, I felt comfortable at this observation. In 'Bion Revisited' (Trist and Murray, 1990), J.D. Sutherland writes: 'As in psychoanalysis, the observer learns to attend to two levels of mental activity: the manifest conscious and the latent subconscious and unconscious.' (p120) By this point in my observations, I was hopeful that I had gained some insight into what was occurring: into the counter-transference, as it were: and the process was becoming more and more natural, I think.

But what of the group's notion of me? What of the transference?

I had long since become someone who happens to attend on Sundays (no questions asked, or few of them anyway); and although I was accepted from the beginning, it was always with relief that I observed with little attention paid to me. Though occasionally someone would speak to me, it was only ever a sentence or two, and usually in a spirit of helping me to understand something that might otherwise have gone unexplained.

Puppy's death was not remarked upon, which surprised me. One might argue: well, what can you say? – as Ms J had remarked in an earlier observation, with reference to a sick horse, 'There's always something sad around a stable' – but all the same, I had expected a mention or two. The group had pulled together to overcome the anxiety caused by Puppy's death, I believe; they had buried their sadness in their work. Perhaps this was why the mood of the Stable was so optimistic and why there was a lot of humour: it was there to protect the members of the group from hostile attacks to the ego. If we follow Freud's theory to its logical conclusion, the very fact that a workforce gels and gets along is a constitution for unconscious tension and anxiety anyway. Add to this the combined sadness surrounding Puppy's death, and we might conclude that this workgroup had unconsciously vowed to block these tensions and to concentrate on being exponents of Bion's *W* (his conceptualisation of work).

'Identification,' writes Wollheim (1971, p.230) 'is the source of the social tie. In virtue of it, members of a group model themselves upon each other, they tend to think and to feel alike, and it is only an extreme variant of this phenomenon that we find in the contagion epidemic in mobs or crowds convulsed by passions of the moment.'

The group at the stable have formed this links of identification, including the comparative newcomers of Mrs N and Miss V. Not only do the horses introject their good objects, the members of the group do too. And if Freud's theory of it being impossible for society to rely solely on love, and that there must be a conflict with love (love being inherently subversive), then the group at the stable are able to endure these anxieties well, sublimating them perhaps into the care of their animals.

A line in my notebook from the day of the eighth observation reads, in total: What would happen if Ellie went? Would the place fall apart? Would the dogs get fed? Would the centre hold?

How swiftly would the group veer towards basic assumption inevitability? Who might pair? Who might be unconsciously coerced into a position of management, however temporary in tenure it turned out? After all, 'a group will unconsciously appoint somebody to do some job they want doing,' says Menzies Lyth in the interview with Pecotic (p.3). And everyone, on the surface at least, has seemed satisfied with Ellie as far as I have seen. As Obholzer writes in the same paper as above: 'Followership is and must be an actively participative process' (p.43). There are other stables in the area for those unsatisfied. Followership is a choice: the group has chosen.

'Can a work group claw itself out of the clutches of basic assumption?' I also wrote, the next day – where 'basic assumption' might be defined as something that the individual does on an unconscious level in order to be part of a group. 'And if so, how?' Who would exhibit high valency, in Bion's terminology; who would exhibit low – where 'valency' describes an individual's willingness to combine with someone else in order to act on the basic assumption. In other words, I suppose I was posing the rhetorical question: would the group fight or flee?

It is tempting to believe, in this case, flee. But whatever the true answer, it is useful to recall Bion (1961, p.118), who wrote: 'there is no way in which the individual can, in a group, "do nothing" – not even by doing nothing.'

Contemporary Response to Observation 2

It occurs to me now that alongside observing the complex eddies of group dynamics and the actions of a competent manager, I was also watching a class in action. Despite the evidence of the lessons that were given at the time, it had always felt more like a place of industry than a place of learning; but now I see that this perception was wrong – or at least only half of the story.

Not only was there the obvious example of my presence there, the purpose of which was specifically to learn; and not only did occasional training sessions take place. It was more than this. It was an atmosphere of near-total immersion: not only was there 'no weather' and not only was it sometimes 'sad', the stable seems to have been (with the benefit of hindsight) a system in balance, not bothered by events in the outside world. It was more than a job or a hobby, it seemed; it was a metaphorical bubble. There were people and animals who needed more than care: they needed their education. Everyone learned from someone else, regardless of the weather or one's personal emotional condition.

It strikes me now that such selflessness is also well-used in a more traditional classroom or workplace setting (or could be). The creation of an environment away from the 'norm' is surely what good education should entail. And perhaps it is our duty to try harder to ensure this bubble holds.

Conclusion

De Board (1978, p.16) writes: 'The basic question which Freud attempted to answer concerns the nature of the social instinct in man. Do human beings form groups and behave in a social manner because of a basic instinct that is "given" by man's very nature and that is, therefore, not capable of further dissection? Or is the social instinct and group behaviour an expression of other, more primary, instincts?'

It is also important to include *Civilization and its Discontents* (Freud 1930, Standard Edition 21) in this context. Freud pondered on whether or not it was too simplistic to envisage 'a cultural community consisting of double individuals like this, who, libidinally satisfied in themselves, are connected with one another through the bonds of common work and common interests' (p.108).

But is it too simplistic a view? In truth, the stable group has perhaps reached something close to this; certainly the model seems to be working.

In a paper entitled 'From sycophant to saboteur – responses to organizational change' (Huffington et al, 2004, p.87) Linda Hoyle writes: 'During any period of organizational change, there is the potential for heightened creativity.' But what does this imply if there is no organizational change? A deadening of the creative spirits? Hoyle continues: 'The anxiety evoked by the process of change can be a major barrier to implementing successful change and it is, indeed, the central tenet of the psychoanalytic theory of the sources of resistance to change.'

Could it be that the stable is something comparatively rare? An organization which attempts to eliminate the need for further decisions via the execution of ritual task performance; an organization in which the workers act as both caregivers and (in a sense) therapists – to one another and to the animals? Perhaps this sounds trite. It remains a fact, even so, that the place has the feeling of a kind of commune. While it is not the case that is share and share alike (as I first imagined for part of my first visit), it is indubitably the case that the people who have worked there for some time have clear impressions of what jobs need to be done and in what order. Much work occurs in silence; or to the accompaniment of the radio's Heart FM. Thoughts that remain unvocalized are nonetheless shared 'telepathically': Freud's theory of Group Psychology made fact, perhaps! The daily repetition of chores is the means by which we might endeavour to reduce psychic excitation; and the same goes for the collective store of excitation in the group.

Caring for horses – what used to be called grooming – is an old-fashioned industry, and it used to be a job for the poor to execute for the wealthy. Accordingly, perhaps, the stable is an environment of stark simplicity – the only amenities available are a flow of water and a few bare bulbs – where there is no telephone and where the only option for communication is face-to-face (or pensive silence). Could it be that these rudimentary qualities are what lend the stable its charms and the enrichment of its emotional life? For there is a lot of emotional life thriving in a stable – or in the stable, at any rate. The humans employ the work of identification, whereby they take an object – a lost object, perhaps, or one that they fear might be lost – into themselves and make it part of their individual and collective inner world, becoming enriched in the process. This object might be the group leader; it might be the horse. Perhaps this notion answers a question of why people keep horses in the first place.

However, might we also propose that the horses enter into precisely the same process of identification? Certainly it would seem the case that the workers calm the horses and vice versa.

But can the stable be a group therapy situation? As Rickman puts it (2003, p.133), 'psycho-therapists are not the only people with a professional interest in the relief of mental pain ...' And doesn't Rickman's definition of group therapy actually ring true of the life experienced at the stable: 'a number of people are assembled together for purposes of explanation of their condition or for exhortation, or for that "companionate therapy" which comes when groups are formed mainly for the purpose of social amenity' (p.134). Or most analogously of all: 'the patient feels that the dignity of his personality and individuality is being respected' (p.140).

That employees now talk to other individuals, rather than interact with a machine, was a fundamental descriptor of work in the post-industrial society; but it is easy to argue that we have gone backwards again, with computer work making long-distance transactions and interactions easy, but at the loss of face-to-face communication. The work done at establishments such as the stable is a return – idealised, impermanent – to a pre-industrial age: in which even the silences speak volumes. The following is from Arlie Russell Hochschild (1983, p.160), and it posits a bleak future:

> If jobs that call for emotional labor grow and expand with the spread of automation and the decline of unskilled labor – as some analysts believe they will – this general social track may spread much further across other social classes. If this happens, the emotional system itself – emotion work, feeling rules, and social exchange, as they come into play in a "personal control system" – will grow in importance as a way through which people are persuaded and controlled both on the job and off. If, on the other hand, automation and the decline of unskilled labor leads to a decline in emotional labor, as machines replace the personal delivery of services, then this general social track may come to be replaced by another that trains people to be controlled in more impersonal ways.

In 'Task and Sentient Systems and Their Boundary Controls' (Trist and Murray, 1990), Eric J. Miller and A.K. Rice define a 'sentient system or group (as) one that demands and receives loyalty from its members'. By this definition alone, but also with the weight of the other evidence I have already mentioned, I would have no hesitation in regarding the stable as a sentient group, and one which it was my privilege to observe and to learn from.

Bibliography

Ballard, J.G. Running Wild. London: Flamingo, 1988.

Bion, W.R. Experiences in Groups. East Sussex/New York: Routledge, 1961.

De Board, R. The Psychoanalysis of Organizations. London: Tavistock Publications, 1978.

Freud, S. The Standard Edition of the Complete Psychological Works of Sigmund Freud. Trans. James Strachey. (24 volumes.) London: Hogarth, 1953-74.

Huffington, C. (et al). Working Below the Surface. London: Karnac, 2004.

Klein, M. Envy and Gratitude. London: The Hogarth Press, 1975.

Likierman, M. 'Psychoanalytic observation in community and primary health care education' in Psychoanalytic Psychotherapy, Vol 11 No 2, 147-157, 1997.

Menzies Lyth, I. 'The functioning of social systems as a defence against against anxiety' in Containing Anxieties in Institutions, Selected Essays Vol 1. London: Free Association, 1988. Originally in Human Relations 1959.

Menzies Lyth, I. The Dynamics of the Social. London: Free Association, 1989.

Obholzer, A and Roberts, V.Z. The Unconscious at Work. East Sussex/New York: Routledge, 1994.

Pectotic, B. 'The Life of Isabel Menzies-Lyth' in Organisational & Social Dynamics 2(1): 2-44, 2002.

Rickman, J. Selected Contributions to Psycho-Analysis. London: Karnac, 2003. Originally London: Hogarth, 1957.

Russell Hochschild, A. The Managed Heart. California: University of California Press, 1983.

Tse-Tung, M. On Practice and Contradiction. London: Verso, 2007.

Trist, E and Murray, H. The Social Engagement of Social Science, Vol 1. London: Free Association, 1990.

Wollheim, R. Freud. London: Fontana, 1971.

Žižek, S. In Defense of Lost Causes. London/New York: Verso, 2008.

Memories: Information, Discovery, Documentary / Georgina Dimmock, Will Hoon and Fiona MacLellan

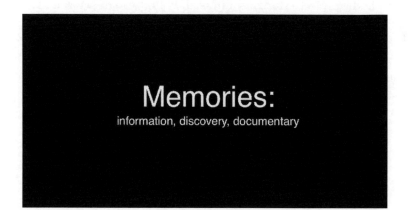

This chapter is in the form of a video at
http://innovativelibraries.org.uk/Memories.mp4

Abstract

Clothes are more than objects that protect us from the elements: they also perform a variety of complex social and cultural functions. They help us encode gender, they shape and present our bodies, they tie us to notions of class and social status and they help us integrate into wider communities and groups. Our clothes also have a further, non-utilitarian function, to both hold and invoke powerful memories. As social beings we gather and collect garments as a way of retaining precious thoughts and we then hoard these in 'wardrobe narratives', thus investing in our clothes yet more layers of extra, totemic value.

In February 2013 University of Northampton fashion and textiles students were asked to create screen-based works that explored and interrogated how we attach memory to garment. Through the act of producing screen-based works each student group went on a journey of research, documentation, creation and dissemination, whilst negotiating a range of methods, actions and processes. Many students captured powerful oral histories that sought to unpack the complex relationships we have with our clothes.

Memories is a short video that incorporates reflections from those involved in the project - students, tutors and library staff - as well as excerpts from the works. It seeks to share pedagogic practice, explore how various agencies within a teaching institution can work collaboratively to support student learning, and to consider how practice and theory can be bridged within the context of art and design education.

'I am what I am': contrasting informational journeys dealing with representations of gay male identity in the 1970s and post-2000s / Antony Osborne

[Please watch Youtube video, 'I am what I am': http://innovativelibraries.org.uk/GG]

How do we become ourselves - the self that we know and others recognise? Family, friends, role models, books, papers, magazines: all have a part to play ... but what if you don't see yourself reflected anywhere? How do you become acceptable to yourself?

This narrative is intended to paint a personal picture of my life as someone growing up gay in the 1970s in a small market town in the North of England where everyone knew everyone else and their business. If you felt different then woe betide you if you told anyone. Physically and culturally it was miles away from a major city, with the advantages and (some) disadvantages that go with that. This journey narrates the way that I sought information to try and make some sense of my sexual identity; from what I read, watched and heard around me.

Clearly, I had an identifiable need for information about health, social events, emotional issues, and not least dealing with family and friends. ('Coming-out' had not yet entered the mainstream vocabulary.) However, there was simply little information to be had.

The library shelves demonstrated a dearth of materials and the social mores of the time prevented open discussion. The few representations in the media were often unflattering, be they either documentary, comedy or newspaper reportage. The lack of availability of literature contrasts with the burgeoning Gay Liberation Movement which was becoming active in the 1970s.

In many senses the information available at the time was very much based on the medical/mental health model from the 1950s and '60s, and reflected the same prejudices.

This is in stark contrast to the 2000s where, in the internet age, there is so much information available that it has become part of a lucrative niche market for those wishing to exploit the 'pink pound'. The willingness of bookshops and libraries to host LGBT sections has brought a wide range of literature to its readers, but could this have contributed to information fatigue amongst its target audience? Is life for a young gay man in the 2000s any different than it was in the 1970s? How does greater availability of information contribute to that?

Certainly there is greater pressure to fit into one of the multiple gay identities that have emerged in the last 30 years, and a growing culture of information avoidance/fatigue that may have health impacts in later years. The homogenous gay 'community' that was struggling to form in the '70s has been and gone, to be replaced by more fragmented communities.

The journey I describe draws on personal experience, books and academic papers on the subject, but remains, at heart, a narrative with links to one or two entertaining/informative snippets scattered throughout.

It is only now in later years, when we are surrounded by so much information, that I realise the dearth of information out there at the time. Initially, I put that down to my geographical location, as rural areas often draw the short straw in these matters. However, on reflection, would my somewhat troubled teenage psyche have been eased had I been able to locate information about health, meet like-minded people, or just feel that someone else had experienced the same thing?

And not to mention ...

The elephant in the room that I need to acknowledge is the AIDS crisis of the 1980s. For the purposes of this piece, I have chosen not to add substantially to the many millions of words that have already been written about it. This is not to deny its undeniable impact on what came after, but simply to acknowledge that it would merit individual study in its own right. Where it has affected information issues I will refer to it as appropriate.

Are you sitting comfortably? Then we'll begin

For those of you old enough to remember, let me transport you back to the 1970s; and for those who are not, let me take you on a magical mystery tour of what seems like a far-off age. In the earlier part of the decade, the country went through decimalisation as well as bread and sugar shortages and power cuts which came about through the 'three day week' in 1972 in anticipation of a miners' strike.

Unconcerned by such matters, the nation's children were riding around on Chopper bikes, and when not doing that, they were bouncing around on large orange spherical objects called Spacehoppers. Failing that they were suffering from bruised wrists from 'clackers', which were all the rage.

By 1977, the Queen's Silver Jubilee, Abba was in the ascendant and flared trousers teamed with platform shoes in the disco were at the peak of their popularity. *Top of the Pops* was one of the biggest shows on the BBC and always the talking point at school, and there was always such discussion about the latest number one single. June 1978 featured a PVC-clad Olivia Newton-John gyrating provocatively with a lithe John Travolta. This seemed to be on the TV for weeks, and for me it made compulsive viewing. At the age of 14, I realised clearly that my belting rendition of 'You're the one that I want' was aimed squarely at John rather than Olivia.

What was a boy to do? How could I deal with this emerging awareness that poked into my consciousness after having lurked in the background for a number of years? Should I try to investigate whether it had a name, or just how wrong these thoughts and feelings were? I needed to find out more; however, plainly I couldn't talk to anyone as that meant admitting it and gave it an external reality. I decided that outward (and inward) denial were the order of the day but vowed to find out more, just out of curiosity, you understand ... but where to look?

Small North Lincolnshire market towns in the 1970s were not renowned for brimming over with information for their inhabitants who might be 'one of those'.

Not being from a 'bookish' background, I made a first foray into my investigation by leafing through a 1950s copy of *Pears' Medical Cyclopaedia* that languished on the bottom shelf of a glass-fronted three-shelf bookcase in my aunt's bedroom. From this, I discovered that the feelings had a name ('homosexuality', which sounded very serious) and was reassured to find that they were just a phase that would disappear in time. It wasn't so reassuring to find the details listed as a medical condition under 'psychiatric illnesses'. I have concluded that the cyclopaedia was wrong, as 35 years later I am still waiting for this phase to pass.

So where else was there to go to find out more? The library seemed like a possibility.

My local library opened for about two hours a night on three days a week and was guarded by the redoubtable Mrs Fogg. We had been taken there on a trip and each was enrolled with the requisite number of pink (!) library tickets. The library was small, and had an adults' and a children's section. It also had its own unique smell of old book and furniture polish. Anyone who broke its hallowed silence by swallowing too loudly or coughing was treated with withering looks from Mrs Fogg. From this description, you will have gathered that it wasn't the most welcoming of places, and certainly discouraged 'out and proud'.

Searching more widely, the local library in a larger neighbouring town had more information in the form of the Kinsey Reports and Masters and Johnson's works on human sexuality. Again, these were very much in the medical/psychiatric mould, and it was worrying to read that I would be likely to live a life outside 'normal' society, plagued by depression and suicidal thoughts.

It seems that these library experiences were typical of those experienced by other gay men at the time and indeed for the previous decades. This lack of information was noted in the 1930s by Porter and Weeks, where one of their contributors notes:

> I now found there weren't many books either. There was a very limited range of knowledge available to you. The books that the

most influence on me were by Edward Carpenter ... I also read J.A Symonds.

(Porter & Weeks, 1991:61)

This lack of information is still prevalent in the 1970s, as Andrew Sullivan states:

> The secret began then when I was young. I hardly dared mention it to anyone; and the complete absence of any note on the subject in my family, or in school, in television, newspapers, or even such books as I could get ahold of, made the secret that much more mystifying. (Sullivan, 1995:6)

The fact is that there was little published material about homosexuality that was aimed at homosexuals themselves. The self-help bandwagon had yet to roll and the material that did exist concentrated on defining it as a disease, and in some cases in suggesting or reporting on 'cures'. The peak time for such 'cures' were in the 1950s, but this approach continued until the '70s. One particular article revisits electric shock aversion therapy that was administered to homosexual 'patients' (Smith, Bartlett, & King, 2004). This article goes on to conclude that:

> The medicalization of homosexuality itself seems to have been the fundamental error, rather than what type of treatment arose as a consequence ... Homosexuality was removed from ICD-10 only in 1992. Our study shows the negative consequences of defining same sex attraction as a mental illness and designing treatments to eradicate it (Smith, Bartlett & King, 2004:427)

As a young man, I was aware from the newspapers that such treatments still went on, and it reinforced the feeling that what I felt (and fought) was completely unnatural and wrong. Importantly, there was a nagging thought at the back of my mind that someday, I might have to go for treatment to stop it. In fact there were times when I thought that I should actually volunteer to go and have the treatment. The whole thing made uncomfortable reading.

What the papers say

Having had little (in fact no) success in obtaining books on the subject, I turned my attention to other media. In actual fact I couldn't really avoid it, as the newspapers in particular were forever screaming about the 'gay explosion'. The papers of the time alternate between the more medicalized word 'homosexual', the older word 'queer', and the newly appropriated 'gay' which was about to make the transition from 'happy'. The Gay Liberation Front was accused of hijacking a perfectly proper English word and using it for its own nefarious purposes. 'Gay' carried political overtones, sandwiched on top of a sexuality that was not deemed to be acceptable for 'normal' society.

In the headlines of the time the press continued to describe the lot of the gay man as one to be pitied, with its imagined sordid sexual hook-ups and, despite the 1967 Sexual Offences Act, fear of blackmail. A few examples of the milder headlines include:

> Southend's twilight world - and the men in fear who haunt it (*Evening Echo*, 21/01/70)

> Doing the Holland Park Walk (*Kensington Post*, 18/06/1976)

> The Gay Explosion (*Sunday Mirror*, 03/04/1977)

Often such articles were followed the week after by readers' responses which allowed the prevailing prejudices of the time to be peddled, despite suggesting that they were providing a balanced view.

With hindsight, some of this is tied up to linguistic devices that would never be allowed in these more politically correct days. For example, *Good Housekeeping* (1972) makes a positive start with the title 'Homosexuals are not a race apart', then proceeds to say that

> no power on God's earth can stem the gut reaction of disgust which homosexuality still arouses in a lot of honest citizens (Mendes, 1972:49)

Surprisingly, this piece ends with a plea to 'honest citizens' to let homosexuals live in social as well as legal peace (presumably by implication, gay men were not 'honest citizens'). Whilst public attitudes towards homosexuality were starting to thaw a little, the implicit message in most media at the time was that gays were good for a laugh or to be pitied, and most importantly that they operate outside 'normal' society, so were of little interest to the public at large (unless of course, someone's husband or son turned out to be gay).

Carry on Camping! - TV representations of gay men

Gay characters started to appear in British sitcoms from the beginning of the 1970s, and this could be considered as a barometer of public acknowledgement of homosexuality. The higher profile of the GLF and the Campaign for Homosexual Equality (CHE) meant that 'the love that dare not speak its name' was seemingly shouting it from the suburban rooftops. In order to be acceptable to the public, however, such characters had to be portrayed in rigid stereotypical terms. Consequently, they were comedy 'poofs' with whom the British public could feel comfortable yet distanced, as they didn't represent any threat to the traditional way of life. These characters came with a pedigree that led back to Julian and Sandy from the radio show *Round the Horne* in the mid-1960s. These two characters had nasal voices, camp demeanour and propensity to use the gay slang Polari, whose real meaning would have been lost on most of its straight audience.

In the blog post '50 Years of Comedy Queers' its author describes how caricatures of gay men were unthreatening because

> poofs mince about, they dress flamboyantly, they have limp
> wrists and camp mannerisms. They may cast a look at an
> attractive, butch man, and indulge in occasional double-
> entendres, but fundamentally, they are asexual and unmanly.
> (Ukjarry, 2009)

Such caricatured behaviours allowed the audience to feel more comfortable with something that remained relatively invisible and the experience of something 'other' outside traditional family life. Acknowledging the existence of gay people as sentient beings would have been uncomfortable.

The poof *par excellence* of the 1970s is Mr Humphries, portrayed by John Inman in *Are You Being Served* (1972-1985). The character of Mr Humphries personified the stereotypical gay menswear assistant , manifested in his high voice and mincing walk with hands either on hips or pressed to his cheek.

Most famously, he was known for his catchphrase 'I'm free!' and his affected, deep, hyper-masculine voice on answering the telephone. Despite the camp persona of the character, both writers and actor always denied that he was gay, but insisted rather that he was simply a 'mother's boy'. Sexual orientation was never made explicit but left hanging in the air for the viewers to decide for themselves.

In another series, *Not on Your Nellie* (1974-1975) viewers regularly met resident queer comedy double act, Gilbert and George, who ran a boutique together. In every episode the ever-silent Gilbert would appear in some flamboyant outfit or other. Hylda Baker would ask "And what are you today then, Gilbert?". Without fail, the same formula was followed each week with Gilbert giving a twirl to which Hylda responded with "<u>Oh you're one of *those*, are you?</u>".

Finally in the pantheon of '70s comedy queens, Dick Emery played the overtly camp and definitely gay character <u>Clarence</u> in *The Dick Emery Show*. As with the majority of other camp characters, the character was formulaic and relied on catchphrases. Clarence would flounce on in a preposterous costume with matching cap, run into a 'straight' man and utter his catchphrase "Hello, Honky Tonks, how are you?". The ensuing conversation led to the customary *double entendres* before he minced off again. The very slight variation from week to week meant that the audience knew what to expect and consequently didn't feel threatened. Such characters as described above would certainly offend today's politically correct brigade, but it has to be remembered that they were of their time.

In 1975, at the age of 11, I somehow managed to be on hand to watch *The Naked Civil Servant* which I had seen advertised in the *TV Times*. It looked set to be shocking, telling the story of Quentin Crisp from childhood to middle age when he became one of the "stately homos of England". I did find it acutely embarrassing as my parents were sitting watching it with me. The reason for this embarrassment stemmed from Crisp's determination to describe himself as (and behave as) an 'effeminate homosexual' (Crisp, 1968). The majority of nascent gay men were not particularly effeminate, a fact noted by an anonymous gay man who wrote to the press in January 1976:

> Being 'gay' means that I am perfectly normal, with one slight difference. I prefer to love another man. I am not, and see no

point in trying to ape a female. There are a great deal like me. (David, 1997:241)

Personally, I found these characters uncomfortable to watch as it made me feel that I had to ensure that I didn't exhibit any such characteristics in case I was 'found out'. The few representations of gay men as either comic/ridiculous or seedy/lascivious inevitably made me feel that I had to avoid being given those particular labels. The enormity of having to live with such a thing and be found out by family and friends was too awful a prospect to deal with. By 17 I had a girlfriend and, whilst feeling that it was wrong for me, I liked the completely different way that people treated me. I had suddenly become 'normal' after spending my life as an outsider looking in. I really can't tell you how good that felt.

At this point, it would perhaps be helpful to remind readers of the LGBT background against which my narrative should be viewed. The period in which I grew up was only about ten years after the 1967 Sexual Offences Act which decriminalised homosexual acts between two men in private providing that they were both over the age of 21. The jurisdiction of the Act did not include Scotland, Northern Ireland or the Channel Islands, nor the Merchant Navy or the Armed Forces. The campaigns for law reform had followed a relatively conservative route and attempted to allow for homosexuals to have respectability, domesticity and discretion. The key aspects of the Sexual Offences Act were in its differentiation between public and private. Whilst this did help some men, there was a vast swathe of others who remained outside the law in terms of where and with whom they took their sexual pleasures.

1970s Gay politics

Most commentators agree that the early 1970s saw the emergence of homosexual consciousness, most readily represented by the use of the word 'gay' as the label for a socio-political movement. This marked a move away from the more medical term 'homosexual' which had started in the nineteenth century. The two predominant movements at the time were the Gay Liberation Front (GLF) and the Campaign for Homosexual Equality (CHE). The former was the more militant and advocated openness, defiance, pride, identity and self-activity. It was based on the model that had taken the United States by storm. The latter was more uncontroversial in its desire to stay well within the law and spend its time trying to build up social facilities for what was now beginning to be called the 'gay community'.

Meanwhile, back in the wilds of ill-informed North Lincolnshire, life and love (or lack of it!) went on in very much the same way as it ever had. I remember seeing double-paged salacious spreads in the *News of the World* about gay scandals involving public figures. My thought was that for something that people found so distasteful, my grandmother (a keen Methodist) was eager to read all about it.

By the end of the 1970s, the 'clone' look was the new way of representing gay sensibilities and to those us growing up at the time it was a welcome alternative to the camp queens so beloved of British comedies. American gay men in particular embraced this hyper masculinity and 'butch' style. They began working out to improve their musculature and grew moustaches combined with short haircuts in an effort to be more 'manly' than straight men. Style-wise, they favoured the 'working man', 'working class rough', 'military man' or 'athlete'. These styles enabled gay men to construct a new identity which rejected the feminine past, as Levine explains:

> Activists rejected the belief that gay men were womanly, claiming that to believe so was a symptom of internalised homophobia (self-hatred based on the dominant culture's view of homosexuality as deviant or immoral). Gay men were simply men who loved men. They were not deviant, were not failed men. They were real men, and in their presentational styles they set about demonstrating their new-found and hard fought conformity to traditional norms of masculinity (Levine, 1998:68)

On the pop scene we were treated to 'YMCA' by the Village People, which epitomises the 'clone' style and look. Despite the opportunities such international changes offered on a micro scale, I would have to have been very confident about wearing such garb to the local disco on a Friday night and of course, I wasn't and would have been laughed at or hit. Nor could I have grown a moustache at that point! The reason for this lack of confidence was the knowledge that in donning this particular 'uniform' you were in effect 'coming out' to all your friends. This was something that was life-changing, needed great consideration, and was totally out of the question for me.

The end of the 1970s saw the opening of the first specialised Gay and Lesbian bookshop, 'Gay's the Word' in the Bloomsbury area of London. Its launch was inspired by the success of gay bookstores in the United States. At that time in the UK, gay related books were not generally available in high street bookshops as they were not felt to be appropriate for the general public. Most of the stock was imported from the United States, for the simple reason that there was not enough 'gay interest' material published in the UK. In 1984 the shop was raided by HM Custom & Excise, under the impression that it was selling pornographic material. A campaign was started which was supported by a number of writers and questions were asked in the House of Commons. Despite this, it would be quite some time before 'gay interest' books would be seen gracing the shelves of High Street booksellers.

Intermission: The 'AIDS Crisis' (a note from the author)

As promised, I will not dwell on this area, but here (http://innovativelibraries.org.uk/ice) are a couple of public information films of the time produced by the UK Government at a time when fear, panic and blame culture were on the rise. The late '80s coincided with the start of my working life and for part of this I worked in libraries attached to hospitals. All the staff had to undergo training for dealing with people with AIDS and as a (albeit closeted) gay man, it was pretty scary to say the least. Hospitals were preparing huge wards for the anticipated pandemic which thankfully never happened in the UK (although, sad to say, it did in some African countries). There were times when the headlines and the TV were blaming gay men for the 'gay plague' and it truly felt like divine retribution. Many of the gains in gay rights that had been made in the 1970s were all but wiped out as public attitudes retrenched against us.

One of the positives to come out of the AIDS crisis in the 1980s was the accelerated development of a 'gay community' which pulled together in the face of adversity and exceedingly negative press coverage. At the time, I was studying for my degree and had fought many demons regarding sexuality before enlightening a few of my closest friends. Once again, I cannot remember referring to any particular literature on the 'coming out' process. This was due principally to the fact that even in my University library books on the subject were still based on the medical model. So ... moving on twenty or so years ...

The 'Noughties' and beyond ...

As someone who works with information, I am only too aware of the colossal changes in information provision and information-seeking behaviour since the inception of the Internet. This has now expanded to include social media such as Facebook and Twitter. These do, I am sure, have significant effects on how people see gay men and how they see themselves, but perhaps it is too early to say what they are. Certainly, for myself, there is always the issue of how much information to include as part of one's online identity. 'Coming out' is not a one-off process, but one that occurs on very many occasions throughout life. This isn't generally in the form of a huge declaration, but simply in either acknowledging or denying aspects of oneself according to each situation. Despite numerous attitudinal changes, we still inhabit a hetero-normative society and not everyone is willing to accept change.

In this section, I offer some of my own thoughts on the information landscape presented to gay men in the 2000s and 2010s and finally attempt to draw some conclusions about the differences with the gay information landscape of my youth.

Some people are gay... Get over it

As discussed earlier, the two main organizations working for gay rights were the GLF and CHE. In the 2000s, one of the best known in the UK is Stonewall which campaigns and lobbies on behalf of the gay community. It has been particularly vocal in the equal marriage debate have a high profile on Social Media. A quick look on Twitter under the hashtag #equalmarriage in summer 2013 reveals vast numbers of organizations and individuals who reveal their thoughts on and support for the Same Sex marriage bill.

In researching this chapter, I have been truly amazed at the sheer volume of organizations catering to the different areas of the 'community' (whatever that may mean). Also, from the dearth of information presented to homosexual individuals in the 1970s, there is an overwhelming variety of materials. One doesn't now have to seek information actively: it is all around, particularly in the social media arena. As with most information, the trick is sorting out the credible and relevant from the incorrect and downright harmful.

Community - what community?

By the 1990s, the combined influence of the political lobbying of the 1970s and the AIDS crisis of the 1980s meant that gay men generally felt a sense of community in the face of adversity. Gay Pride marches became regular events on the calendar and there was an increasing trend towards 'gay villages' in some cities (Manchester's Canal Street area, for example, which featured in the 1999 series *Queer as Folk*). The Gay community had been transformed into the LGBT Community (Lesbian, Gay, Bisexual and Transgender). The rainbow flag was adopted as a symbol of the diversity of this community in 1978 and its continued use in the 2000s shows how it has retained its symbolic importance to the gay community. The very notion of a 'community' of gay people is something that would certainly have been foreign to me in the 1970s. It is something that one can choose to embrace (or not as the case may be). There are still many MSMs (men who have sex with men) who feel that their identity is outside the 'gay' community. Even so, in the 2000s, they can obtain health and social information from regional offices of MESMAC, which is set up for all men, however they identify themselves.

By the early 2000s, I was living a Northern city which boasted a couple of gay pubs which expanded and flourished into the 2000s. When the financial crisis hit them, several closed. Nearby, however, in Leeds and Sheffield were larger gay 'scenes' and the Northern gay mecca of Manchester was not far away. They all boasted their drag nights, stripper nights, and even 'camp' bingo and quiz nights (the camp stemmed from the fact that the questions were read by drag queens). There was always a mixed crowd with men of a variety of ages. This helped to foster a sense of community and in many senses resonated with historical accounts of closed 'Gentlemen's clubs' in the 1930s and '40s. The key thing was that I had a choice to engage or not.

In the 1970s in my home location there was no choice, as venues were non-existent. I have always maintained that the further East across the country you travel, the fewer gay venues and facilities there are.

'Gay' becomes more mainstream

The 1990s saw the introduction of niche books and magazines aimed at gay men. This has continued into the 2000s and it is now easy for a gay man to read gay fiction, romance, porn, sexual instruction, self-help - in fact any conceivable thing they could wish for. In the UK, Waterstones has a 'Gay and Lesbian' section in many of its shops. However, there is a counter-argument from the gay community that the sexual orientation of either the author or chief protagonists should not be enough to define a genre and therefore place it in a separate section from those items intended for the heterosexual community.

Searching on the Internet, there is a London gay book group and individual lists of 'good reads for gay men'. So much choice - the lists are endless - but do people have time to read them? Also, I suspect that the quality of many of them leave something to be desired.

What were some of the reasons for the gay information explosion in the late 1990s and beyond? Personally, I would attribute it primarily to the increasing visibility of gay people which meant that there was suddenly a new niche market for advertisers. A new and relatively affluent consumer group had been created and everyone was keen to benefit from the 'pink pound' and the lifestyle it represented. One such magazine which straddled the millennium is *Attitude*, a magazine that appeals to a wide age range of gay men. It is aspirational in style and assumes a certain level of income and similar preoccupations. Generally the cover features an attractive (and generally heterosexual) sportsman or actor that is of interest to the gay 'community' with a full interview inside. Predictably for a magazine aimed at a gay audience, there are extensive sections devoted to fashion, film and music . In addition, it flirts with the pink pound with numerous pages of swimwear and underwear. As a by-product of such advertising, the nature of the product also doubles up as an excellent opportunity for handsome men to appear in various stages of undress.

One very positive aspect that I respect about this magazine is that it looks at gay life holistically, and provides advice about relationships which helps to address the increasing sexualization and commodification that I will discuss later.

Health-wise there is a regular column from an HIV positive contributor as well as 'The Clinic' with Dr Christian Jessen (the gay TV Doctor from Embarrassing Bodies) and 'Body Talk' which looks at the body issues, diet and exercise regimes of ordinary readers. As a source of information, *Attitude* is articulate and informative ; indeed, the June 2013 issue is themed as a 'youth' issue specifically aimed at younger gay men, and deals with many questions that I would dearly love to have had answered (or even acknowledged) when I was in my teens.

Health information is an area where (at least on the surface), the 2000s are way ahead of the 1970s and yet, despite this, the Stonewall report about the health of gay and bisexual men makes depressing reading. Of particular concern to me are its findings about mental health, eating disorders and body image as well as sexual health and HIV status. Could it be that a new hedonism has gripped younger gay men, who are not so aware of the 1980s and all that it represented, and are intent on having a good time? Additionally, the concentration on HIV means that some men are more complacent about other STDs that are 'curable', thereby increasing the numbers suffering from them. Somewhat worrying, I feel.

Are you coming out?

If there is one area where information has burgeoned since the 1970s, it is the vast range of information about 'coming out', whether that be in book, magazine, or video clip/internet form. This process was encouraged in the 1970s as a way of making the sizable, but silent, minority of gay men more visible to society at large. It was not, however, purely a '70s phenomenon, since self-disclosure of sexual orientation as a way of changing public opinion had been advocated by Ulrichs in 1869.

Coming out in the 70s was a major thing with the potential to change your life (and as far as I could see, not necessarily for the better). Given the shift in social attitudes today, it is a more accepted 'rites of passage' process for gay people, but that does not mean that it is easy. A project called It gets better was started in the USA in 2011 in response to the number of teenage suicides among those werebullied for being gay, or perceived as being gay, by their friends. It uses video clips by gay adults who try to assure the younger people that it does actually get better over time, that the bad times will pass and that they are not alone. Such campaigns on the internet are linked with social media so that those who may need such information are more likely to be aware of it via their customary media use. Even if that information is not pushed out to them, it can be located by searching the internet.

For those contemplating the coming out process, a voluminous literature of 'coming out tales' has gradually formed its own sub-genre and from these can be gleaned useful tips on what to do and what not to do. Importantly, the reader becomes aware that they are not the only one tackling this issue: that they are treading a path that has been trodden by many before. Individual circumstance and the irrevocable nature of coming out mean that it is always momentous; however, there is much more help at hand than there ever has been in the past. A great example is in the above-mentioned June 2013 issue of *Attitude* which features a whole section on coming out. In his editor's letter, Matthew Todd explains:

> It's not a question of screaming or shouting or 'defining yourself by your sexuality', as some people seem to think - it's just about being real with yourself and the world. Often we don't come out because we think other people's reactions will be bad, when sometimes it is our own reaction we are scared of. (Todd, 2013:8)

Gay identities online: the influence of Gaydar and Grindr

One of the difficulties faced by gay men has always been that of how to locate and meet like-minded people, particularly if one was born in areas away from cities and towns with their own 'underground' gay community. From the 1900s, gay men would test the sexuality of potential conquests or friends through their understanding and recognition of Polari, which enabled gay-centric subjects to be discussed without being comprehended by the straight majority. It was one way of marking out a gay identity. This gradually fell out of use in the 1960s and was replaced in the early 1970s by the 'hanky code' whereby sexual preferences were indicated by different coloured handkerchiefs worn in the back pocket.

In the 2000s, the most significant influences on the lives of gay men across the world have been the rise of online dating sites. The number of gay dating sites has proliferated in the 2000s and much newsprint has been devoted to their pros and cons. Of the many available, Gaydar and Grindr are good representatives of this particular type of site.

Gudelunas recognizes that:

> Generally, we know that people can enhance their sense of group belonging and social identity by using media that features people who belong to the same social group. This is particularly a key in the case of 'invisible' sexual minorities like gay men who grow up and experience life both with the ability to 'pass' as heterosexual and who most typically grow up with no immediate gay family members. (Gudelunas, 2012:353)

Gaydar started in 1999 and is popular in the UK, Europe, Australia and North America. It offers gay men the chance to create a profile and meet others in online 'rooms'. These may be based on geography, thus facilitating local meets or arrangements in advance, or according to specific sexual likes or dislikes, for example 'suits', 'humiliation', 'older men' etc. It also has rooms for bisexuals and married men. Both of the latter may or may not identify with the 'gay' community in a physical sense, yet the internet gives them the opportunity to explore new sexual horizons with relative ease. In all cases, it allows the user to decide what aspects of their sexual persona to reveal.

The other key player is Grindr. Launched as recently as 2009, Grinder already has 5 million members across the world, with over 350,000 users in London alone. Unlike Gaydar, Grindr works via mobile devices and uses geo-location to locate gay/bisexual/bi-curious men in the vicinity. You can use it to locate potential partners who may be sitting or standing only a few metres away from you!

Such dating sites may be seen as liberating. However, in many ways they go against the whole idea of the gay community. As one regular user of Gaydar reports:

On the one hand, it does link people up, but they are not socialising, they are not meeting in bars. They are just sitting talking down a line, ordering what they want, when they want it. That can be a very narrow thing. (Addley, 2007:25)

Such has been the success of these sites that in recent years, the fortunes of the bars in Manchester's famous Canal Street have taken a real downturn. This has been attributed to the use of online dating to meet rather than physical meetings in its bars.

In some ways, I find that the worlds of Gaydar and Grindr give a narrow view of what gay life could/should/can be. Young gay men venture into these worlds and soon become part of the culture which is seemingly predicated on sex, size of equipment, having the perfect body and not being over the age of 35 if you want any attention. Little wonder, then, that gay men are more prone than straight men to issues around body image, depression and substance abuse. Few people can be perfect enough to live in these worlds for long. As someone with a fair amount of life experience I can see how this online culture works, but despite this, there is part of me that can sometimes feel like an 'outsider' again in the same way that I was an 'outsider' from the much more fiercely hetero-normative world of my younger years. In fact, I sometimes rejoice in the fact that I do not have to participate.

Where are we now?

As I look back, having been partnered for 20 years and 'Civil Partnered' for five, it is difficult to believe how much things have changed since my boyhood. If someone had told me then that I would be able to have a gay relationship recognised in law by the State, I would have said 'impossible' - and yet here we are. Not only that, but the Same Sex Marriage Bill is currently passing through the various stages of its parliamentary journey. In numerous countries in the world, same-sex marriage is being recognised. Indeed, France has just celebrated its first gay marriage. As we have seen, however, many people think that this is a step too far and it has caused rifts and protests in many areas of society. Ironically, the early activists in the gay liberation movement would have been horrified at the drive for same-sex marriage, as marriage represented the existing social structures that they wanted to change. Could it be that the drive for same-sex marriage that has been enthusiastically espoused by numerous gay organizations stems from a need to have gay identity identified and 'approved' by the state? Perhaps this reveals a seam of low confidence and self-esteem in the gay populace?

Also in the UK, the Equalities Act (2010) enshrines anti-discriminatory legislation in law, thus protecting many minorities from both direct and indirect discrimination. Surely this must be a good thing, as bullying in whatever form has always been a problem and continues to be so.

Despite all the excited tweets about same-sex marriage, we should not be coerced into thinking that everything in the gay garden is lovely. The majority of information that people use to help form their opinions is trumpeted from official sources, and is based very much around the premise that society has become predominantly 'metrosexual' and therefore accepting. This is not necessarily the case. In 2008, the BBC reported that 'gay' was the playground insult of choice. Such use of the word to imply 'rubbish', 'second class' and 'pathetic' takes us right back to the equivalent insults with which I was familiar in the 1970s. Is it a case of *plus ça change*? ... However, dear reader, I digress.

'What a culture we live in. We are swimming in an ocean of information, and drowning in ignorance.' (Evans)

Whether we agree with the implied cause and effect in this statement, we cannot deny that we are swimming in an ocean of information. I started this information journey way back in the 1970s in describing the dearth of information to me as a young gay man growing up in rural North Lincolnshire. Certainly, for me that was problematic, but like us all, I was a product of my time and learned to find my own way in the best way I could. The lack of information - and the often negative information that was available - was reflective of the society in which I lived. Does information reflect societal attitudes or does it create and reinforce them? Information in itself is neutral and dispassionate, but the way it is portrayed in the media is bound to be influenced by those who place it there whether in word or image.

As I have worked on this piece, I have come to realise the seismic nature of information provision embodied in the internet. Yes, this has affected everyone - but perhaps it has affected less visible minorities more than most, in that it enables them to interact with others on a virtual level. While this is helpful in some ways, it seems that they lose a sense of what it is like to interact in the physical world. Some men report that the almost immediate sexual contact following online meetings can feel like it's still online and they actually get confused between the two. I worry that the way that such online cultures have developed are damaging to those whose are trying to deal with their sexual identities. Nevertheless, they follow the pack because that's what they feel is expected of them.

As this is a retrospective description of my personal information journey, it would be inappropriate to make too many generalisations about the differences between the two information eras that I have discussed. My personal view, however, is that I would have benefitted from having access to magazines like *Attitude* and to the wide variety of health information to be found on the internet. Also, it would have been good to have been able to contact others so that I didn't feel quite so much of an alien being. Who knows: I may have used the 'coming out' stories too.

Ultimately, even with all the information in the world, construction of sexual identity in an internal process only partially informed by external factors. There is a large literature on identity construction which I don't propose to go into. I do believe that in the 2000s, however, the increasing 'normalisation' of gay identities as part of mainstream society must be of benefit in reducing the feeling of the 'outsider' whose lot in life would previously to have lived on the margins or to have created an almost psychotic double identity and live in the constant fear of blackmail. Perhaps the need for a 'gay community' has lessened as we have become more integrated. Who is to say that gay identities will not go the same way and that being gay will be accepted as simply a different way of being?

So I have reached the end of my journey of discovery. It has been a surprisingly emotional one: I have remembered all sorts of people and situations that have passed into my personal 'deep storage' and have been retrieved kicking and screaming to the forefront of my mind. If you have read this far, I thank you for your patience and hope that I haven't seemed over self-indulgent. If I have been, then I hope you will understand. Whilst it doesn't define me, it certainly plays a large part in being the person that I am ... and after all, this is my life !

References & Bibliography

Addley, E. (2007, 17 February 2007). Saturday: Let's talk about sex: Gary Frisch, who fell to his death last week, founded a dating website that transformed gay men's lives. . *The Guardian,* pp. 25-25, from http://search.proquest.com/docview/246638010?accountid=11526

Armitage, G., Dickey, J., & Sharples, S. (1987). *Out of the Gutter: A survey of treatment of homosexuality by the Press.* London: Campaign for Press and Broadcasting Freedom.

BBC. (2008). How 'gay' became children's insult of choice. Retrieved 18 March 2013, from http://news.bbc.co.uk/1/hi/7289390.st

Blake, L. (1970, 21 January). Twilight men of Southend. *Evening Echo*

British Pathé. Gays & Lesbians in the 50s 60s 70s. from http://www.britishpathe.com/workspaces/rgallagher/Gays-and-lesbians-in-Britain- 1950s-1960s-1970s Retrieved 19 March 2013

Bundred, D. (2012). Gay Fiction. Retrieved 18 May, 2013, from http://danielbundred.blogspot.co.uk/2012/12/gay-fiction.html

Crisp, Q. (1968). *The Naked Civil Servant.* London: Jonathan Cape.

Cullen, T. (2003). HIV/AIDS: 20 years of press coverage. *Australian Studies in Journalism, 12,* 64-82.

David, H. (1997). *On Queer Street:A Social History of British Homosexuality 1895-1995.* London: Harper Collins

Davies, N. (1979, Aug 22, 1979). Gay harassment 'widespread' says CHE

Dodds, C., Keogh, P., & Hickson, F. (2005). *It makes me sick : Heterosexism, homophobia and the health of Gay men and Bisexual men.* SIGMA research.

Edwards, N. (2010). *Queer British Television: Policy and Practice, 1997-2007.* University of Nottingham

Evans, R.P (2013). *A Step of Faith.* New York. Simon and Schuster

Guasp, A. (2011). *Gay and Bisexual Men's Health Survey*: Stonewall.

Gudelunas, D. (2012). There's an App for that: The Uses and Gratifications of Online Social Networks for Gay Men. *Sexuality & Culture, 16*(4), 347-365.

Isay, R. A. (1989). *Being Homosexual: gay men and their development.* London: Penguin.

Kendall, C. N. (2004). *Gay Male Pornography: An Issue of Sex Discrimination*: UBC Press.

Levine, M. P. (1998). *Gay macho: The life and death of the homosexual clone.* New York: New York University Press.

Meem, D. T., Gibson, M. A., & Alexander, J. F. (2010). *Finding Out:An introduction to LGBT studies.* California: Sage

Mendes, J. (1972, October). Homosexuals are not a race apart. *Good Housekeeping,* 49.

Mills, R., Trumblach, R., & Cock, H. G. (2007). *Gay history of Britain:Love and sex between men since the middle ages.* Oxford: Greenwood World Publishing.

Porter, K., & Weeks, J. (Eds.). (1991). *Between the Acts:Lives of homosexual men 1885-1967.* London: Routledge.

Pullen, C., & Cooper, m. (Eds.). (2010). *LGBT Identity and online new media.* Oxford: Routledge.

Roberts, S. (2011). Exploring how gay men manage their social identities in the workplace: The internal/external dimensions of identity. *Equality, Diversity and Inclusion: An International Journal, 30(8),* 668-685.

Ryland, P. (1976, 18 June). Doing the Holland Park Walk. *Kensington Post,*

Sender, K. (2005). *Business, Not Politics : The Making of the Gay Market: The Making of the Gay Market.* New York: Columbia University Press.

Shepherd, S., & Wallis, M. (1989). *Coming on strong: gay politics and culture.* London: Unwin Hyman.

Slaughter, J. (1970, Feb 1, 1970). The men who still feel hunted. *The Observer*

Smith, G., Bartlett, A., & King, M. (2004). Treatments of homosexuality in Britain since the 1950s--an oral history: the experience of patients. *BMJ, 328(7437),* 427.

Sullivan, A. (1995). *Virtually Normal: An argument about homosexuality.* London: Picador.

Todd, M. (2013). Editor's letter. *Attitude:The Youth Issue,* 8.

ukjarry. (2009) Fifty years of Comedy queers, *Streetlaughter: a gay cavalcade of comic stereotypes*

Weeks, J. Wolfenden and beyond: the remaking of homosexual history. In A. Bingham, L. Delap, S. Sheard & P. Warde (Eds.), *History & Policy: Connecting historians, policymakers and the media*

Weeks, J. (1977). *Coming Out:Homosexual politics from the nineteenth century to the present.* London: Quartet.

Wikipedia. LGBT rights in the United Kingdom. from http://en.wikipedia.org/wiki/LGBT_rights_in_the_United_Kingdom

Wikipedia. GLF in the UK. from http://en.wikipedia.org/wiki/Gay_Liberation_Front

Wikipedia 1970s in LGBT rights, Available from http://en.wikipedia.org/wiki/1970s_in_LGBT_rights

Wikipedia. Timeline of LGBT history. from
http://en.wikipedia.org/wiki/Timeline_of_LGBT_history_in_Britain

Wikipedia. Campaign for Homosexual Equality. from
http://en.wikipedia.org/wiki/Campaign_for_Homosexual_Equality

The Library / Bryony Ramsden

1. Finding.

Flora realises she is lost not when the canopy begins to obscure the sunlight, but when the roots of the buildings begin to seemingly purposefully trip and obstruct her path. She withdraws further into her hood, and on looking down to check her footsteps, notices breadcrumbs. They have evidently been there for some time, sodden from rain, blackened with mould; but they are definitely there, and appear to be leading the way along a track. Looking up, Flora can just see through the buildings to a warm glow in the darkness, some way down the trail. The paper in her hand suggests that she need not go hunting for help as it will find her, but so far she's not had much luck in getting any. She may as well follow the crumbs, so she shuffles down the trail, hoping that the level of deterioration of crumbs does not equate to false leads. She realises she is hungry: she isn't sure how long she has been lost, but it seems long enough to develop hopes that the fresh version of the crumb source is available at the end of the trail.

With some difficulty, she navigates to the source of the glow. It's a building, but different to the ones she's already passed. It appears to be huddling itself into a nook between the roots of the others, but is nevertheless daunting in its presentation thanks in part to the way it contrasts so much with its surroundings. She's read about places like this before: they beckon you in with promises of warmth and comfort, you let your guard down, and then next thing you know, you are fighting off surprisingly hairy sweet old ladies whose brooms turn out to not just be a tool for sweeping. However, the temptation is too great, and this isn't a story told to small children to ward them away from strangers or those whose eyebrows meet in the middle, so she moves closer. The front of the building is broad, and the glow she saw at the start of the track is still the same soft warm light, filtering through small windows. The door is wide, bright, and open, with smells of cinnamon and coffee, and something bitter she can't quite identify, snaking their way into her nostrils. She pauses, glances around, and gives in. What other option does she have, really?

On entering the building, Flora is surprised to find it filled with bright colours. Considering the external view, the inside is a high contrast. Six-foot-high sofas, giant chairs, stools you would need a stepladder to reach, throw cushions and for some reason, tiny low tables (that couldn't possibly be reached from the seating) populate the room. But no inhabitants: Flora feels very alone and conspicuous here. The smell of coffee is stronger, but there is a marked lack of cups, and yet some … staining … on the furnishings. It looks sticky and uninviting.

"Hello."

Flora turns with a start to see a tiny figure on one of the cushions. What she initially thought a button is a small bear.

"You need something?" the bear asks.

"I'm lost, but I think I've found where I was told to go."

The bear tilts its head to one side, and presents what can be assumed to be a furry perplexed expression. "Why did you come here?"

"I was told it was the place to go for help?"

"What kind of help?"

"I don't know, just … help."

"Who told you to come here?"

"They said I could find things out here."

"Do you often follow instructions from others without knowing what you want?"

Flora is both irritated and confused. Maybe she made a mistake.

"Do you ever respond with anything other than a question, Mr … ?"

The bear sighs. "I am The Bear. I provide guidance. To provide guidance I need to know what is required as an answer."

"But I don't know the answer! That's why I came here!"

The Bear suddenly appears to increase in size and stature, shows his teeth, and growls "Then I cannot help you if you cannot answer me." He turns, returns to his original size, and snuggles into the cushion with a snort.

Flora isn't quite sure what to do next, but it's warm in here, and so she concludes that she can probably do considerably worse than progress deeper into the building. She turns down what she assumes is a corridor, and finds a large rusty metal gate. Through the gate, she can see about ten metres away that there is a bright area, with lots of movement and what she interprets to be light-hearted noise. She decides it would be a good place to get to. However, the gate is somewhat off-putting. Why is it there? Is she not meant to go that way? The Bear didn't suggest that she couldn't go anywhere, but then to be fair The Bear wasn't really very helpful. So maybe it won't do any harm to just try pushing the gate a little bit ... Flora leans gently against the metal. It seems to give a little. She pushes a little harder. Its resistance appears to be more based on rust than a lock, so she puts all her weight behind it, and it swings open with a loud squeal.

"You could have asked to come in, you know!" the gate exclaims.

The movement and noise further into the building has noticeably reduced. Flora feels momentarily guilty, until she realises that there is nothing to suggest she should ask. "I would have asked had I known that was all I needed to do! I'm sorry!"

"Hmmmm," the gate ponders. "I'm not sure that it is necessary to know to ask, given that a gate implies entry, and more so a gated entry implies a requirement to request to enter. However, this place is for anyone who may enter, and entry is allowed to those who require it, and if you require entry, then that is what is the important matter in this case."

Flora begins to wish that she had never bothered leaving home, given that those she has met have so far been rather confusing, and only very partially helpful. But Flora is not one to give up, whatever she might feel might be there to give up on, which in this case, she isn't quite certain about. She thanks the gate for opening, and tries to be as nonchalant as possible as she strolls towards the source of the noise.

She enters a large, open, brightly lit and colourful area, with very little furniture compared to the other side of the gate, which is good as it would get in the way: there's lots of movement here. People! At last, people! Lots of people are running around looking very busy indeed. They move around the area flocking from multiple doors to space to corridor, in what appears initially to be randomly, but as she observes more, it begins to strike her as highly organised and purposeful. She dare not stop them to ask what they are doing in case she ruins things. A few metres ahead of her is a desk covered with papers, with a bear seated at it, in front of a set of shelves containing heavily handled textbooks, some dirty cups (one of which has a picture of the bear with a paw around the shoulder of someone vaguely recognisable on it), and a large bushy plant. The Bear! Flora can tell she is clutching at familiarity when she finds she wants to go to speak to someone as unhelpful as The Bear again, but this place has so far been very overwhelming, and a known entity, no matter how problematic, is better than nothing. She runs across to The Bear and greets him.

"Hello!"

The Bear smiles at Flora. "Hello! How may I assist you?"

Flora is surprised. This is quite different behaviour to what she saw earlier. "I'm not sure, to be honest. I've not really got any further than when I saw you ten minutes ago."

"Excuse me? I don't think we've met before?"

"But we were just talking on the other side of the gate?!"

"Ahhh! That would be my colleague, The Bear. I'm The Other Bear, but feel free to just call me The Bear if that's any easier for you."

Flora feels she really ought to try and get used to feeling totally confused by this place and its inhabitants.

"OK ... Oh, but then maybe you can help me! I've been sent here, and I'm not really sure what I'm looking for, but I was told that this was the place where I'd find help."

The Other Bear smiles. "Of course! However, I can't give you the answer, as that would be telling."

"Oh ... But I don't even know what I'm asking really, so how do you know?"

"I know. Trust me, I know. But to give you the answer would be inappropriate, so you'll have to find it out yourself. I can tell you *how* to find the answer though, or where. Is that OK?"

Flora ponders. This is probably the best she'll get for now. "OK then. Either or both of those would be good, thank you."

"In that case, you find the answer through that door over there. How you get it is up to you, but I'd recommend you use the steps outlined on the wall once you get through the door. Thank you, come again!"

"But what if …"

"Thank you, come again!"

"But how do I …"

"Thank you, come again!"

Flora sighs. This is definitely the best she is going to get. She looks towards where The Other Bear is pointing. Lots of the busy looking people keep running in and out of the door there. She looks back towards The Other Bear. He is very busy brushing his ears, and obviously doing his best to ignore her. He peeps up from behind his brush at where Flora still stands, starts, and quickly goes back to grooming himself. The door is not getting any quieter, so Flora looks for a gap in the flock, and makes a run for it.

2. Searching.

Behind the door feels like an entirely new place. While people seemed to be rushing in and out of the door on the other side, this area is hushed, and there is very little movement around the area. Rows and rows of wooden tables and benches run the length of the large, softly lit room. The walls are covered in dark wooden panels, with no windows. Anyone visible is sat on a bench with their head bent onto the table, their arms folded beneath their forehead. Flora has a barely controllable urge to start jumping up and down on the tables, or drumming on them. She looks around for the instructions The Other Bear referred her to. On the wall next to her is a piece of glass and above it embossed gold lettering providing 'instructions':

Think.

Think again.

Think a third time.

Write a query based on a combination of base 6 numbering and binary, with appropriate written interjections as suits the query (ensure interjections are in Assyrian cuneiform or C++).

Input query using screen below.

Oh. Flora feels quite put out. She can't even see any way of 'inputting' her query on the screen, but at least she's thinking more about that rather than the query itself, which she has absolutely no idea how to write. And knows no C++ or cuneiform (Assyrian or otherwise). And has a poor grasp of different methods and bases of counting. Flora looks around. Everyone at the tables appears to be motionless, and she dares not ask them any questions. She takes a step towards the screen, creating a thunderous boom with her (soft-soled) shoes. The room's inhabitants look up at her with disgust and agitation, stare at her indignantly for a few moments, and as one lay their heads back on the tables, tutting like clocks as they do so. This is not good. She begins to crouch down so that she might crawl across the floor on hands and knees to avoid noise, and gets knocked backwards by an oddly silent runner heading towards the door. She just manages to see a flash of him rushing out of the room, hair flaring out behind him as he runs. How did *he* manage not to disturb anyone? And he's the first person she's seen even moving around in this room – where did he come from?! She carefully rotates herself from her rear to her knees, and notices one of her pockets seems to have something in it. There is some kind of calculator type device there now, with a note.

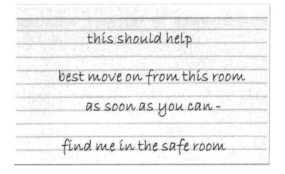

this should help

best move on from this room

as soon as you can –

find me in the safe room

Puzzled, Flora looks at the device. It is like a calculator or a small computer, but with images on the keys instead of letters or numbers. Several of them look quite reassuring and friendly, so she tries pressing a picture of a helpful-looking dog, a mouse pointing at some cheese with a happy face while rubbing its tummy, and a door with an exit sign above it. The device's screen flickers on, shows some kind of calculation process, then flashes with a collection of numbers, symbols and letters. Flora slides across to the glass. As she approaches it lights up with a panel that - thankfully - has a set of keys including what is displayed on the device screen. She types them in, the glass glows blue, and a small piece of paper comes out of the bottom of it. It says

```
................What you need is HERE....room 23945
....shelf 9206....item 180967025....................
....Please note charges are sometimes applicable....
```

With some relief, Flora crawls carefully towards the door, and moves out as fast as she can.

She feels oddly glad to be back in the fast, busy movement of the entry area. At least here she doesn't feel like she is being disruptive. Or not much anyway. So where is the room she needs to visit? What makes it safe? Should she go back to The Other Bear? She decides she doesn't really have much option but to try and ask.

"Excuse me, please could you direct me to a room I need to find?"

The Other Bear looks up, and evidently decides this is an appropriate question. "Of course! Where is it that you want to go?"

"The safe room?"

The Other Bear looks briefly shocked, but quickly recomposes himself. "I would not advise you to visit The Safe Room. Contrary to its name, it is not safe. Additionally, visiting The Safe Room may result in charges."

"But isn't that my choice to make?"

"Perhaps, but I cannot be held responsible for your actions, and will not do anything to advocate such actions, and therefore will not tell you where it is." The Other Bear spins around on his chair, the plant rustling as he does so. "No! I will not tell!"

Flora is not surprised by the lack of help, but is surprised by the vehemence of the response. So what to do now? Is there anyone else to ask? *Lots* of people, but all carefully ignoring the conversation she has just had. She wanders towards a corridor.

"Not that one!" someone whispers. "Go through that red door over there."

She looks towards the whisper, and sees a young woman making busy by the wall next to the corridor, looking at her from the corner of her eyes.

"Thank you!" she whispers back, and heads towards the door. It is marked with lots of signs:

Staff advise against entering this door

PLEASE USE ALTERNATIVE ROUTES
OR ACCESS POINTS

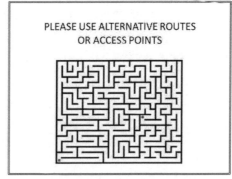

BEWARE:

NOISE POLLUTION

The institution will not be held responsible
for anything that happens beyond this door.

Clearly someone does not want people to use this door, but there is
nothing to say anybody cannot actually enter it: just that they would
prefer it wasn't used. The decision takes little consideration: Flora tries
the handle, and the door swings open freely.

Through the door is a long, blandly painted corridor. Flora follows it. It
seems to continue round corner after corner with no other doors
leading from it. Flora continues along it for some time. Then reaches an
abrupt end. Still no other doors. Was the girl who told her to come this
way wrong, and the signs right? But there doesn't appear to be
anywhere to go! She starts to head back the way she came, but as she
turns, she notices something odd with the wall to her left. It looks
wrong, but she can't quite say why. It looks kind of wobbly, like heat
rising from concrete. Slowly, she reaches forwards and tries to touch
the wall, but there is no wall there to touch. There is an alcove masked
by the paintwork and something else Flora can't identify. The simple
fact of it being meant to be hidden or disguised by someone makes her
want to investigate further, so she tries walking into the alcove, and
spies the corridor continues a few metres to a door.

As she reaches the door, she can see there are letters on it, painted the same colour as the door, as if to hide them. They say

THE SAFE ROOM

Well, that wasn't *too* bad really, but she would never have found it if the girl in the entry area hadn't told her to go this way. She tries the handle. It turns, and the door easily swings open away from her.

What is behind the door is both wonderful and terrifying. This is what she had been hoping for. The room is large, with filing cabinets, desks, a coffee machine next to a cake stand, and potted ferns dotted around the area. It feels immediately like this place is useful, or rather more useful than everything else Flora has encountered so far, but she isn't sure what she needs to do now she is here. Flora wanders around the room, a little overwhelmed, takes a piece of cake, absentmindedly brushing the leaves of a small potted beech tree as she passes it, and browses cabinets as she munches. Then hears a voice.

"You made it! I'm so glad!"

Flora turns to see who she assumes to be the young man who gave her the note. He is slim but broad-shouldered, with a head of long thick spiky green hair. She finds herself smiling for the first time in a while.

"Thank you for the ... thing that helped me do the search."

"You are welcome. I don't like to see people go through what I had to. I've been here too long to want to see that anymore."

"How long *have* you been here?"

"Long enough."

"You look tired. Are you OK?"

"I *am* tired, but I can't leave now. I've set down too many roots here to just go and lose all the progress I've made. There's a small group of us who are working from here, and one of them makes very good cake, so I'll keep going as long as there's food and drink here!"

"Mmmm, it *is* good!" although Flora thinks that cake isn't really enough to make her want to stay here any longer than she has to. "So I have to find something now. I have information on where this thing is, but I don't really know where to find it now."

The man sighs. "I'm afraid all I can do now is point you in the right direction of where the materials are kept."

"You mean it isn't in here?"

"Nope. This is just information we've been collecting about where things might be. We don't actually know a lot, but we know how to make the device I passed you. Can I have that back by the way? We don't have many of them, but there are lots of people who need help with that terminal as much as you did."

Flora passes the device back to him. "Thanks for lending it to me. I'm not sure I used it right, I just punched in what felt like I wanted."

He smiles "That's just what you should have done! It was designed by the lady who brews the coffee for us. She wanted it to be as intuitive as possible without having to think about it, and she'll be glad it seems to be working."

"I'll let you know if it is, when I find what the numbers are pointing me towards! So where do I go to find this?"

He looks at the piece of paper. "Hmmm. That's one of the smaller warehouses, luckily. I think ..." He opens a filing cabinet, flicks through the tabs in the drawer, and checks it against Flora's paper. "Mmmm. Not quite the warehouse I was thinking of, but it is still one of the smaller ones. You'll need to head back down the corridor, through the yellow door, and all the way to the end. There's a door marked 'Items for retrieval 6' there. That's the one you want."

"Thank you, I really appreciate it! So why is this room so hidden? Why does it seem to have so many signs telling people to turn back?"

The man sighs. "It helps protect us from the bears, but also the bears are more likely to let us stay around if we aren't too ... overt in our work." He looks down, and Flora senses this is not a conversation to continue. She thanks him for his help again, and takes the long trip back down the corridor to the yellow door.

3. The Answer.

Flora, not without trepidation, enters the room the green-haired boy directed her to. Shock. Fear. Confusion. Flora assumes this is a room, but she cannot see a wall at the far end, or even a far end to the room, nor a ceiling. Before her are piles of books. Many piles of books. They climb as high as she can see, the bases of them many metres wide. What happened to the shelves? There is light from somewhere, which allows there to be some visibility, but where to start? The numbers on the paper appear to be meaningless; she crumples it up into a ball and plays with it anxiously in her hand. Where to start?! What to do?! She wanders towards the nearest pile. There must be thousands of books in it. Even if she finds the right pile, what if the book is at the bottom of it, underneath all the others, hidden? Exasperated, Flora folds into a heap, and leans her head against the books behind her.

Wait!

What was that she saw moving in the corner of her vision just then? There is it again! And there's a noise, a whirring sound. Trundling around the corner, there appears a large robot on wheels. On its head is a bulb flashing on and off, its face covered by a mask of a 'smiling' bear.

The robot halts in front of Flora, spins around surprisingly agilely, and beeps. Flora waits a little. It beeps again. Then it waves a metal arm a little irritably, and presses a button on its chest.

"Sorry about that, I forgot I was still set to my own language," the robot says apologetically. "Do you need anything?"

"Yes!" Flora leaps up excitedly. "I need to find this!" She smooths the paper out in the hope it is still readable, passing it to the robot. The robot examines it carefully, presumably through eyes hidden behind the bear mask.

"Hmmmm. This is a little damaged, you know. I might have to charge you."

"That's OK, I'm getting a bit desperate now. Can you help me?"

The robot stares at the paper.

"Yes, I believe I can. I can certainly at the very least assist you with locating where this item is placed. You have come to the correct room, but this will take a little travelling to reach." The robot twists round, revealing a plate protruding from its back. "Please seat yourself behind me, and fasten the seatbelt. Secure all loose items and or belongings. Should a crash occur, place your head between your knees and pray to ZZZZ INSERT APPROPRIATE DEITY HERE ZZZYYP for forgiveness."

Flora climbs on, and almost immediately the robot speeds away, light flashing. Several times it abruptly turns at a ninety degree angle and continues in a different direction, to the point that Flora wonders if she'll be able to find her way back to the entrance. After a few minutes, the robot jolts to a halt and announces "We have arrived. Thank you for travelling with 'Bearfaced Flights'. Please consider our services for your next travel needs."

Flora unbuckles the seatbelt and collapses in a bundle to the floor, somewhat relieved. Looking around, she sees they have actually barely moved from where she entered the room. She decides not to bother asking about that.

"So where do I look for 'my' item? How do I find it now I'm in the right place?"

The robot raises an antenna from behind its mask, and points it towards the top of one of the piles. "For your convenience, the item you require is placed on top of this selection. You will need to retrieve it from there."

"How do I know which is the one I'm looking for though?"

"It is the large orange book. I am sure you will manage to locate it."

And with that, the robot zooms off, light flashing.

Flora takes a deep breath. It appears she will need to do some climbing to reach the item. She isn't sure how to do this, but clearly there aren't many other options. She tentatively places her right foot on what appears to be a stable section of the pile of books. It seems sturdy enough. She moves her left foot to join it. Nothing bad happens. She repeats the process. She gains a little confidence. She climbs a little higher, and a little higher. It is at the midpoint of the pile that she realises something is wrong. While the pile is still standing, she seems to be moving away from the top of it. She looks down and sees that the base is expanding as books rapidly move downwards and somewhere at the bottom there must be some kind of liquid as the books are turning into what looks like soggy *papier-mâché* and it is effectively becoming the information equivalent of quicksand, so the only way Flora can go is up. She pushes upwards and climbs and climbs and her shoes slip off but she doesn't care, and she uses her toes to push further up but she can't push any more as there is nothing but papery sludge to push against and she is sliding down and she can't move as the slurry of paper is sucking her in and she doesn't know what to do and now she is up to her waist and she can't feel any floor even though she is nearly that far down again now but wait. The boy from the Safe Room is here. He is moving towards her and he takes her hand and heaves but the slurry doesn't want to let her go and he heaves on her arms again and she wonders how he can manage to stand on the mush and she sees that his feet are much broader and more wooden? than they should be but that doesn't matter now as she is moving and he's pulling her OUT of the mess and she is FREE, and he lifts her up, and places a book on her and she sees it must be the one she needs and he carries her out of the room. And the people and The Other Bear all stare at them as he walks by the desk area, and the people cheer and The Other Bear looks irritated and Flora notices rather oddly that there seems to be a plant missing from behind the desk now, but that doesn't matter as they have beaten it, whatever it is, and they have the answer, and he carries her out of the building with the answer to use as they see fit and

STOP. Wait. Is that right? TRY AGAIN.

Flora takes a deep breath. It appears she will need to do some climbing to reach the item. She isn't sure how to do this, but clearly there aren't many other options. She tentatively places her right foot on what appears to be a stable section of the pile of books. It seems sturdy enough. She moves her left foot to join it. Nothing bad happens. She repeats the process. She gains a little confidence. She climbs a little higher, and a little higher. It is at the midpoint of the pile that she realises something is wrong. While the pile is still standing, she seems to be moving away from the top of it. She looks down and sees that the base is expanding as books rapidly move downwards and somewhere at the bottom there must be some kind of liquid as the books are turning into what looks like soggy *papier-mâché* and it is effectively becoming the information equivalent of quicksand, so the only way Flora can go is up. She pushes upwards and climbs and climbs and her shoes slip off but she doesn't care, and she uses her toes to push further up but she somehow feels her toes getting longer and her hands seem to be able to grasp the ledges better as her fingers seem longer and she climbs and she climbs and pushes ahead and she's at the top and she grabs the book that is probably the one and she leaps. She leaps, and lands on solid ground with the book in her hand. Or what was a hand, but now seems to be developing into a set of twigs. Her feet are acting in the same way, her toes lengthening into little root-like tubers. Oddly, Flora doesn't feel that this is a surprise, or a bad thing. She strides into the entry room and passes the desk and The Other Bear stares at her agog and the people all stare at her in awe and she strides by them and lets them see that she HAS THE BOOK and they clap and nod or bow to her as she passes them and she leaves as she can now that she has the answer and she has found out what she needed to.

STOP. Hold on a moment. That still isn't quite right.

She pushes upwards and climbs and climbs and her shoes slip off but she doesn't care, and she uses her toes to push further up but she somehow feels her toes getting longer and her hands seem to be able to grasp the ledges better as her fingers seem longer and she climbs and she climbs and pushes ahead and she's at the top and she grabs the book that is probably the one and she leaps. She leaps, and lands on solid ground with the book in her hand. Or what was a hand, but now seems to be developing into a set of twigs. Her feet are acting in the same way, her toes lengthening into little root-like tubers. Oddly, Flora doesn't feel that this is a surprise, or a bad thing. She strides into the entry room and passes the desk and The Other Bear stares at her agog and the people all stare at her in awe and she strides by them and lets them see that she HAS THE BOOK and they clap and nod or bow to her as she passes them and she leaves as she can now that she has the answer and she has found out what she needed to.

But she doesn't leave. She stops, and goes back. She knows what she needs to do. She places the book gently on the desk, and The Other Bear shrinks away from her, looking down hiding his eyes. She notices the plant from behind the desk is missing, but the pot is still there. She runs her 'hand' through her hair, and finds it to be sprouting leaves. This seems like the right place, but it isn't her place, and she needs to move quickly now. She leaves the area, and heads to the Safe Room again. There's no problem reaching it now. It is clear she no longer has anything to be afraid of. She lifts her now bulky feet into the room, and finds a corner. The corner. An empty pot. She finds herself a comfortable position, and waits. She knows she won't need to wait too long.

A note.

Flora's experiences are inspired by personal observations as librarian and as student, drawn from experience of many institutions, and from sharing experiences with peers who have often observed and dealt with similar behaviour and interactions. The students, the bears and the setting are not directly attributable to any specific individuals/institutions, and should not be interpreted as representations as such. I should also emphasise that this isn't necessarily representative of what librarians do, or how they behave, but how students can perceive their experiences of using a library and their interactions with any library staff, not just librarians (all library staff are librarians in the eyes of many who visit them).

This story would not have existed were it not for the help of many people, but in particular, Becky Gregson-Flynn who reminded me that fairy tales are good, and Helen Walker and Shannon Robalino who helped provide obscure or difficult languages for the search method.

Editors' note

The maze graphic on page 228 is © Nevit Dilmen, from Wikimedia Commons

An Endnote

We've cast our net wide to catch our contributors and hope that we've brought you at least a taster of what information literacy means in all its breadth and variation. Has this book made you think? Edified you a little (or a lot)? Advanced the idea of information literacy at all?

If so, feel free to carry on the conversation! Use the hashtag #InfoDiscovery on Twitter (Emma is @LibGoddess and Andrew is @andywalsh999 if you want to follow us) or comment on the blog (http://innovativelibraries.org.uk/wp/).

Illustration by Josh Filhol for "The Fishscale of Academicness".